Pitt Cue co.

THE COOKBOOK

THE COOKBOOK

{ CONTENTS }

FOREWORD
BY
{ APRIL BLOOMFIELD }

. . . .

Perfecting barbecue (BBQ) is a slow process. It takes time to get it right. From smoking a whole hog to finding the perfect sweet-to-spicy ratio in a sauce, it can take years to reach satisfying results. In the American South, BBQ is something of a bragging right. Families hold decades-old secret recipes dear to their hearts. Considering the commitment and individuality of a truly great BBQ recipe, it is inspiring when a new restaurant introduces something distinctive and delicious. The undertaking is even more impressive when the restaurant isn't in the US, as most are, but in London.

Pitt Cue, by far, serves some of the most refined BBQ I have ever eaten. Simply put, the meat is cooked to perfection. The smoke is elegant and the meat is so juicy and tender that it melts off the bone with each bite. I appreciate the English charm that comes through in the manageable portions served on white-enameled trays with sides served in pickle jars. Delicate but packed with flavor.

I really appreciate Pitt Cue's take on BBQ. You can tell that they care. It is especially obvious in the way the hickory chips have been burnt off to just the right point. It's that moment when you see the thin blue line of smoke with its intoxicating aroma and all that's left is the sweet layered smoke that has gently laid itself over the copious amount of beef ribs, pork shoulders, and sausage. Pitt Cue makes one of the most amazing sausages, almost like cotechino; delicately smoked and lightly charred. And the spicy short ribs are something I often crave. They are cooked in a spicy-yet-sweet vinegary sauce with hints of overly blackened peppers that makes them moreish and totally addictive.

There is no mistaking Pitt Cue's attention to detail. The pride they take in the food they produce is reflected in all the recipes they share with you here. This book will be loved again and again and the pages will undoubtedly be coated with the sweet, smoky residues of tenderly made BBQ. And who knows, maybe some of the recipes will become family secrets of your own.

. . . .

THE | # INTRO

Before Pitt Cue

At some point in history our ancestors discovered that meat tastes better when cooked, and soon after they worked out that grilling is best done over the glowing coals of a dying fire. The evolution of man is intrinsically linked to cooking meat over fire. The manipulation of fire by Homo erectus provided early humans with warmth, protection and a point of social contact, but most importantly brought with it a radical change in the way dinner was served. Our ancestors had the means to evolve only so far until they realized their ability to cook hunks of animal meat to make it digestible, and with this massive change in the way we could assimilate protein our brains grew considerably. Barbecue is unequivocally the oldest form of cooking and is quite possibly the very thing that made us human!

Barbecue as we know it sprouted from the Caribbean in the form of barbacoa and was spread by Spanish explorers throughout the region. They also introduced the pig into the Americas which in itself is a pretty awesome achievement, and the American Indians in turn introduced the Spanish to the concept of true slow cooking and preserving with smoke. Eventually this smoking went from a method of cooking or preserving food to a way of flavouring food when these Spanish colonists settled in South Carolina, and it was in that early American colony that Europeans first learnt to prepare and to eat 'real' barbecue. During this period, poverty in the Southern states of America meant that every part of the pig was eaten or saved for later including the extremities and offal, and because of the effort to rear and cook these hogs, pig slaughtering was a time for celebration and merriment, and the neighbourhood would be invited to join in.

If only more of these gatherings were seen today. These feasts were called 'pig pickin's' and traditional Southern barbecue continued to grow out of these gatherings.

Every part of the Southern United States has its own particular variety of barbecue, particularly concerning the sauces, but also extending to the cuts, spice rubs, wood and types of meat they use. But of course, barbecue is not solely a culture and cuisine of the US, it is a technique used all over the world, the very first technique to be mastered in fact! Almost every culture and country has their own form of barbecue, from the asador found in northern Spain, the asado in Argentina, the ocakbasi of Turkey, or robatayaki in Japan. All these forms of barbecue inspire and inform us and we are guilty of that very British tendency for mixing styles from wherever it is we feast and fatten ourselves.

Our First Year

In 2011 Tom and Jamie formed Pitt Cue, named after the small village where Tom grew up near Winchester. They started with very few expectations, and seemed destined for failure. Everything kept going wrong, and had they not developed an invaluable talent for 'winging it' the history of Pitt Cue could have been a lot shorter. The smoker was stopped at customs (apparently they had to check no families or bombs were hiding inside) and arrived the day before they were due to open. Given the fact that our pork shoulders needed a solid 15 hours to cook, this was a significant cock-up. It was promptly housed under a DIY rickety lean-to in the back passage of a friend's deli.

KELSO NUT-BROWN LAGER.   COTTRELL OLD-YANKEE ALE   SIXPOINT VIENNA PALE   CAPTAIN LAWRENCE LIQUID GOLD   WANDERING STAR MILD HEART   CONEY ISLAND PILS.

It was sod's law that the café across the road was a vegan stronghold with many of the surrounding residents members of the dark side. Those divine meaty smells that our smoker put out through the night were not so enticing apparently. It would be nice to think we converted some people with those smells. In reality, very few of them saw the light and we had weekly complaints. Even those residents of the meatier sensibility kicked up a stink as we kept them awake with middle of the night pork prep, washing up sessions and Captain Beefheart stuck on repeat.

The second-hand catering trailer was twice the size as expected, and our shitty 4x4 compiled the already mounting problems when she gave up the ghost the night before opening. Fortunately, an RAC recovery vehicle took pity on us. About a week later than anticipated we opened the trailer's hatches for the first time on Friday 20th May; fortunately there had been enough group texts and emails to guarantee some custom.

Slowly but surely Pitt Cue gained a following on Twitter which in turn solicited the attention of some influential London-based bloggers and then gradually the ladies and gentlemen of the press caught wind of our pig meddling. There were all-day parties, all-night parties, some terrible public dancing, daily sell-outs, an unhealthy amount of staff picklebacks, no sleep whatsoever, collaborations with some brilliant restaurants and people, and we even managed to stop the trains from Charing Cross to Waterloo after the billowing smoke from our half-drum jerk barbecues was seen through the railtracks. At the end of the summer, Pitt Cue had been reviewed in publications as diverse as the *Evening Standard* and *Eurostar*

magazine, and more importantly had amassed several thousand followers on Twitter, a loyal army who turned out regularly throughout one of the most miserable summers on record to eat pig, bosh picklebacks and Fernet Brancas and listen to a some horrendously amateur busking on the South Bank (we were very close to throwing one particularly painful bag-piper into the Thames) while getting soaked under the most porous bridge in London. After that initial summer trading on the South Bank, we teamed up with a few of those regulars, Richard of Hawksmoor, and Simon and Andy of The Albion, to help us grow up a little and open a bricks-and-mortar restaurant in Soho in January 2012.

Pitt Cue is now barely a year old, very young to be writing a cookbook perhaps, but these recipes are just a little snapshot of some of our first year, combined with an articulation of our attitude towards food and farming, an attitude that seems to prevail today. The attitude of anything is possible and that rules are there to be broken, or at least bent a little, as long as the results are super tasty.

While researching for the restaurant, we travelled extensively throughout the Southern United States in search of inspiration and lots of bourbon. We found barbecue to be localized, much the same as Italian food is regionalized, and were amazed at both the quality and variety of food to be found. Most significantly perhaps, our travels confirmed that trying to replicate US barbecue was exactly the route we did not want to go down. We just needed to carry on cooking food that we enjoyed eating, keeping it simple and using the very best British produce to do so.

Barbecue is affected by many variables and this is what makes it such a challenge to nail, as well as what makes it interesting. Although our recipes suggest cooking times and temperatures, the reality is that these will soon become irrelevant, little more than rough guidelines, when you get going on your own barbecue and using the meat you have sourced yourself.

Your barbecue and your meat will be different from ours and this is just the first variable to consider. Our meat recipes should thus be taken as a guide to how to approach your barbecue. Barbecue is a technique, just as poaching, baking and frying are techniques, and should be approached similarly. If you source the very best meat for your daily cooking, do the same when cooking with fire and smoke; if you buy the lesser cuts of meat for braising and long slow roasting, do not feel you have to change this habit on the barbecue. The practice of sourcing meat should not change for a new technique and this is perhaps the most important thing to take on board. When you combine grilling and smoking with stunning meat there is very little that needs to be done above and beyond to create a brilliant meal. We have eaten great barbecue all over the world but the best meals are repeatedly had at the tables of those who put the sourcing and the provenance of their produce up there with the skills they use to cook them.

Although our recipes are often simple, the real work started quite some time ago, on an expanse of beautiful green countryside or woodland where the animals are free to roam, root and frolic. In this book you'll see our own animals that are reared in Pitt, in the woods (our 'Pigtopia') running free to forage – Pitt Pigs if you will – and at the time of writing we have already taken many to their final destination and served them in the restaurant. The results of our labours have proved jaw dropping, as far removed from any pork we'd ever cooked as can be; a revelation.

By the time this book is published we will have a sizable herd of pigs, producing what we believe to be the best pork in the country. We hope to be rearing all our own pigs for the restaurant in the near future. It is, for us, the only way to guarantee that the very best pork into the restaurant each day: pork as it once tasted from pigs living the lives they deserve to live.

It takes time for an animal to grow and although modern farming methods and breeds speed things up, this makes for the kind of flaccid tasteless mush that can be found on the shelves of your local supermarket. We strongly encourage you to source the best possible meat you can and to engage with your local butcher. The future of small dedicated farmers really does hinge on us buying better meat.

Next

We have ambitions to rear and keep a fold of Highland Cattle: Pitt Beef. We also want to open more Pitt Cues, not identikit copies but restaurants with the same philosophy of sourcing and cooking style, each one very different but connected. Watch this space.

Tom, Jamie, Simon and Richard
January 2013

DRINKS

DRINKS

· · · · · · · · · · · · ·

ALL BOURBON IS WHISKEY NOT ALL WHISKEY IS BOURBON
{ A VERY, VERY BRIEF HISTORY OF BOURBON }

· · · · · · · · · · · · ·

Bourbon is an unsung hero, the under-appreciated and undervalued stepchild of the spirits world, and Pitt Cue is out to change all that. It is the quintessential American liquor, with roots that go straight back to the men who shaped the country: George Washington made it, as did Abraham Lincoln's father – and it even provoked America's first civil war, the Whiskey Rebellion of 1791–4, sparked by a tax on distilled spirits levied to help pay for the War of Independence. Amazingly, it took George Washington more men to put down an army of whiskey distillers than to defeat the British: no wonder Americans have had a love affair with the spirit ever since.

In a strange twist of fate, it was the Scots and Irish, fleeing famine and religious persecution in the British Isles, who brought distilling techniques to North America. But there, too, they faced an anti-Catholic society, so as soon as they could, many continued west. In what is now the modern state of Kentucky, these settlers were given land as part of a government incentive as long as they promised to grow corn. Naturally, they used this to make whiskey. For this reason, we have

one of the few remaining wholly corn whiskeys on our list.

The name 'bourbon' derives from a county within what is now Kentucky. It takes its name from the French royal family, in recognition of the assistance the French gave the Americans during the War of Independence. Ah, the irony.

There are various people credited as being the first to distil bourbon – Elijah Craig and Evan Williams being favourites; however, no one really knows, and to name a single person is fanciful. What is true is that in Kentucky the settlers found a land flowing with pure, alkaline water from limestone deposits beneath the soil. The spirit that flows from the stills is clear and is known as 'white dog mash' (a version of which we also stock behind the bar) so called because it is clear and has a bite like a dog. It was this that was drunk before the whole process of barrel ageing was developed. Surplus whiskey distilled in Kentucky was placed in barrels to be sent south down the Mississippi River to places such as New Orleans. Legend has it that the barrels were stamped with the word

'Bourbon' to designate their origin... Whatever the truth of that is, the intense heat of the American South – combined with the duration of the transit and presumably additional storage time – led people to discover the maturing and mellowing effects of keeping the spirit in barrels. Like many food and drink legends, whether Champagne or Roquefort, the discovery was a happy mistake. Later, the practice of ageing the whiskey in charred barrels became common and set us well on the way to modern bourbon.

It is claimed that the characteristic properties of ageing spirit in charred oak were discovered at a time when the only barrels available to whiskey makers were those that had been previously used to store salted fish, and to get rid of the smell they charred the inside of the barrels. The longer the maturation in barrel, the more flavour and colour is imparted to the bourbon. But there are two downsides: first, if left too long in a barrel, the bourbon can become overly woody and unpleasant tasting. Second, the longer bourbon remains in a barrel the more spirit is lost to evaporation and leakage. Typical maturation periods range from two years upwards. Currently, we stock bourbons that have been aged for as many as ten, twelve, eighteen or more years in barrel.

With the proliferation of distilleries came the growth of movements to put them out of business. The temperance movement whipped the churches into choruses of disapproval and led directly to the Prohibition Act in 1919, when the consumption of alcohol was almost universally banned in the United States: see *Boardwalk Empire* for details. Entrepreneurial man that he was, Jamie's grandfather resorted to making 'bath tub' gin, which might have contributed to his early death. During this time, most Americans who found a way to continue drinking had to rely on the lighter-flavoured whiskey that was smuggled in from Canada, which meant that the more strongly flavoured bourbons and ryes fell out of fashion when Prohibition was repealed in 1933.

From the beginning of Pitt Cue, bourbon has been a crucial part of our menu. Well before that, it's fair to say we've long been drawn to bars, and Jamie in particular has always felt their irresistible allure. As a child, he spent Christmas and Easter in the French Alps, always staying in the same hotel. Being the only child of a single mother, somewhat more used to the company of adults than his peers, the bartender let him stand behind the speed-rail, help out a little bit and generally watched him ply his craft. Social services would have had a field day. On Jamie's twelfth birthday, his mother gave him a bartender's handbook, a cocktail shaker, a marble slab and two cases of spirits – and told him to get on with it. The rest, as they say, is history.

SOME WHISKEY TERMS

BOURBON
A whiskey with a corn content of between 51–80% is classified as bourbon. The remainder of the formula can be made of rye, wheat, malted barley or malted rye.

RYE
Rye is another form of American whiskey but must be made from at least 51% rye, the other ingredients of the mash being, typically, corn and barley.

SINGLE BARREL
A whiskey for which each bottle comes from an individual ageing barrel instead of being created by blending together the contents of various barrels to provide a consistency of colour and flavour.

SMALL BATCH
This rather unspecific term is meant to induce greater confidence in the consumer because the contents of a relatively small number of selected barrels are combined, but as there is no set parameter for the term it is pretty meaningless...

STRAIGHT WHISKEY
Any whiskey that has been aged for a minimum of two years in charred, new oak barrels is a straight whiskey. All of the bourbons served at Pitt Cue are straight whiskeys.

THIS TWO-SHOT DRINK DOESN'T REALLY QUALIFY AS A COCKTAIL, BUT IT IS SO INTEGRAL TO PITT CUE THAT THERE IS NO WAY WE CAN LEAVE IT OUT. IT BEGAN LIFE IN NEW YORK, WHERE A SHOT OF JAMESON'S IRISH WHISKEY WAS 'CHASED' WITH A SHOT OF PICKLE JUICE. THE IDEA BEING THAT THE SAVOURINESS OF THE PICKLE JUICE ACTS TO NEUTRALIZE THE EFFECTS OF THE HARSHNESS OF THE WHISKEY ON THE THROAT AND TASTE BUDS, PREPPING YOU READY FOR ROUND TWO AND BEYOND. WE OPENED THE PITT CUE TRAILER WITH BOURBON PICKLEBACKS AND THESE SHOTS RAPIDLY BECAME SYNONYMOUS WITH OUR BUSINESS.

THE PICKLEBACK

SERVES 1

bourbon	35ml
Our Pickle Brine *(see page 78)*	25ml

These two shots are to be taken in quick succession, the whiskey first and then the pickle juice. We prefer a smaller shot of pickle juice … we also recommend trying the juice from other types of pickles: pickled beetroot juice looks splendid and pickled pear juice is festive in the winter months.

THE BOILERMAKER

AGAIN, NOT STRICTLY A COCKTAIL, BUT NO LESS DELICIOUS FOR THAT. THIS DRINK EXPERIENCE COMBINES A GLASS OF BEER AND A SHOT OF WHISKEY AND IS SAID TO DATE BACK TO THE BARS THAT CLUSTERED AROUND THE STEEL MILLS IN THE HEYDAY OF THE AMERICAN INDUSTRIAL BOOM. THE COMBINATION PROVIDED JUST THE RIGHT BALANCE OF REFRESHMENT AND INTOXICATION REQUIRED BY THE MEN WHO CAME OFF SHIFTS IN THE SWELTERING FACTORIES.

SERVES 1

bourbon	35ml
draught beer	½ pint

Some people pour the shot into the beer, some even drop in the entire filled shot glass, but we prefer to chase the shot with the beer.

—MANHATTANS—

RATHER LIKE ALMOST EVERY CLASSIC COCKTAIL, THE ORIGINS OF THE MANHATTAN ARE LOST IN THE MISTS OF TIME, IN THIS CASE THE NINETEENTH CENTURY. ESSENTIALLY IT CONSISTS OF A SPIRIT AND RED VERMOUTH — THE ARCHETYPAL VERSION INVOLVES RYE WHISKEY, AS THE GREATER SPICINESS IS BETTER ABLE TO DO BATTLE WITH THE OTHERWISE POTENTIALLY OVERPOWERING VERMOUTH.

THE MANHATTAN

SHOULD THIS CONCOCTION SEEM A LITTLE TOO AUSTERE, ADD A SPOONFUL OR TWO OF THE SYRUP FROM A JAR OF MARASCHINO CHERRIES TO MAKE THE DRINK SWEETER, A SO-CALLED SWEET MANHATTAN. YOU CAN ALSO EXPERIMENT WITH DIFFERENT TYPES OF BITTERS — PART OF THE JOY OF MAKING COCKTAILS IS DISCOVERING WAYS TO TWEAK DRINKS TO MAKE THEM MORE TO YOUR OWN TASTE.

SERVES 1

rye whiskey	50ml
sweet vermouth	25ml
Angostura bitters	a dash

GARNISH

maraschino cherry or orange slice (or both)

Assemble all the ingredients in an ice-filled tumbler and stir to ensure that they are mixed and chilled.

Garnish with a maraschino cherry or a slice of orange (or both), and add two straws.

BIG MAC 'N' RYE

THE J-DAWG

THIS IS POSSIBLY THE FIRST PITT CUE COCKTAIL — DEVELOPED ON THE TRAILER IN MAY 2011. INSPIRED BY THE DIRTY MARTINI, WHEREBY SOME OF THE LIQUOR FROM A JAR OF PICKLED ONIONS IS ADDED TO THE DRINK, OUR PICKLE JUICE IS ADDED TO A CLASSIC MANHATTAN. THE SAVOURY SWEETNESS OF THE PICKLE JUICE CREATES A DRINK THAT WE BELIEVE COMPLEMENTS THE FOOD WE SERVE IN A MOST DELIGHTFUL WAY. SOMEONE WHO ONCE TRIED THE DRINK COMMENTED THAT IT TASTED SIMILAR TO THE SAUCE USED ON A BIG MAC, AND SO THE NAME WAS BORN.

THIS RUM MANHATTAN WAS NAMED AFTER JAMIE BY COLIN GRANDFIELD, ONE OF THE BARTENDERS AT PITT CUE, A JOKE THAT STUCK ... WE USE A VERY DELICIOUS AND RICH DARK PANAMANIAN RUM, WHICH IS AGED IN USED BOURBON BARRELS (SEE THE THEME?) AND HAS A SWEETNESS THAT MAKES THE ADDITION OF MARASCHINO SYRUP OPTIONAL. HOWEVER, ALWAYS EXPERIMENT WITH THE FLAVOURS, AND IF YOU THINK THAT THE DRINK COULD DO WITH AN INCREASE IN RICHNESS, FEEL FREE TO ADD SOME.

SERVES 1

rye whiskey	50ml
red vermouth	25ml
Our Pickle Brine *(see page 78)*	a dash
Angostura bitters	a dash

GARNISH

orange zest or slice

Assemble all the ingredients in an ice-filled tumbler and stir to ensure that they are mixed and chilled.

Garnish with orange zest or a slice of orange, and add two straws.

SERVES 1

dark rum	50ml
red vermouth	25ml
orange bitters	a dash
Angostura bitters	a dash

GARNISH

orange slice

Assemble all the ingredients in an ice-filled tumbler and stir to ensure that they are mixed and chilled.

Garnish with a slice of orange, and add two straws.

CUE JUMPER

RED RYE

THIS IS A DELICIOUS VARIANT ON A MANHATTAN, USING BOURBON (WHICH IS SLIGHTLY LIGHTER THAN RYE WHISKEY) AND POMEGRANATE PICKLE JUICE. IT STARTED OUT AS A PUN IN SEARCH OF A DRINK, BUT AFTER USING SOME LEFTOVERS FROM A BATCH OF PICKLED POMEGRANATE, IT ALL CAME TOGETHER. THE PICKLED POMEGRANATE JUICE IS LIGHTER AND LESS HEADY THAN OUR REGULAR PICKLE JUICE AND YET DOESN'T LOSE ANY RICHNESS. IT IS A MARVELLOUS DRINK, WHICH, ALAS, WE SELDOM HAVE ON THE MENU, AS THERE ISN'T MUCH CALL FOR PICKLED POMEGRANATES.

THE RED RYE IS A CLASSIC MANHATTAN AUGMENTED BY THE ADDITION OF FERNET BRANCA. AH, FERNET … JAMIE IS ALWAYS IN SEARCH OF A WAY TO GET THIS AMAZING AMARO INTO COCKTAILS TO JUSTIFY ITS PRESENCE ON THE BACK BAR, WHERE IT NEEDS TO BE BECAUSE ITS REVIVING PROPERTIES ARE OFTEN CALLED UPON, IN THE FORM OF SHOTS, DURING THE COURSE OF THE DAY. THESE AND OTHER MEDICINAL PROPERTIES LED TO THE SALE OF FERNET REMAINING LEGAL DURING THE ERA OF PROHIBITION IN THE US.

SERVES 1

bourbon	50ml
red vermouth	25ml
juice from Pickled Pomegranate (see page 197)	25ml
Angostura bitters	a dash

GARNISH

orange or blood orange slice

Assemble all the ingredients in an ice-filled tumbler and stir to ensure that they are mixed and chilled.

Garnish with a slice of orange or blood orange, and add two straws.

SERVES 1

rye whiskey	50ml
red vermouth	25ml
Fernet Branca	12.5ml
Angostura bitters	a dash

GARNISH

lemon slice

Assemble all the ingredients in an ice-filled tumbler and stir to ensure that they are mixed and chilled.

Garnish with a slice of lemon, and add two straws.

SOURS

POSSIBLY THE MOST POPULAR STYLE OF COCKTAIL AT PITT CUE,
SOURS COME IN A WIDE VARIETY OF GUISES; BUT LET'S START
AT THE BEGINNING.

WHISKEY SOUR

ONCE THE SWEETNESS, OR OTHERWISE, OF THE LEMON JUICE IS TAKEN INTO ACCOUNT,
THE AMOUNT OF SUGAR SYRUP YOU ADD IS ALL A MATTER OF TASTE, BUT WE FEEL
THAT BOTH SOUR AND SWEET SHOULD PLAY AN EQUAL PART AND NEITHER ONE SHOULD
DOMINATE THE OTHER. THE ANGOSTURA BITTERS ADD A DELICIOUS, ALMOST NUTMEGGY
RICHNESS TO THE DRINK. THE TRICK IS TO SHAKE THE COCKTAIL FIERCELY TO DEVELOP
FROTH ON TOP WHEN IT IS POURED INTO A GLASS.

SERVES 1

bourbon	50ml
lemon juice	50ml
Sugar Syrup *(see page 56)*	a dash
Angostura bitters	a dash
free-range egg white	¼

GARNISH

lemon slice

Shake all the ingredients hard in a Boston
shaker with ice, then strain over ice in
a tumbler.

Garnish with a slice of lemon, and add
two straws.

NEW YORK SOUR

THE NEW YORK SOUR WAS THE ONLY COCKTAIL FRAN ASTBURY, OUR BAR MANAGER, INSISTED THAT WE HAVE ON OUR DRINKS MENU WHEN WE OPENED IN JANUARY 2012. VISUALLY IT IS A DELIGHT, AS THE RED WINE BLEEDS INTO THE CREAMY SOUR BELOW. THE TRICK HERE IS TO POUR THE WINE SLOWLY DOWN THE LONG TWISTED HANDLE OF A BAR SPOON. THE DIFFERENCES IN THE SPECIFIC GRAVITIES OF THE WINE AND THE SOUR ARE SUFFICIENT TO SUPPORT THE WINE ON TOP. CAREFUL EXPERIMENTATION WITH THE SWEETNESS OF THE SOUR IS REQUIRED, BUT THE DILEMMA IS THAT THE ONLY WAY TO ENSURE THE WINE FLOATS IS TO MAKE THE SOUR OVERLY SWEET. IN THE END THE DRINK WILL PROBABLY BE MIXED TOGETHER, SO THE RESULTS OF ALL YOUR EFFORTS WILL BE, AS EVER, TRANSITORY.

SERVES 1

bourbon	35ml
lemon juice	35ml
Sugar Syrup *(see page 56)*	a dash
Angostura bitters	a dash
red wine	50ml

Shake everything except the red wine in a Boston shaker with ice, then strain over ice in a tumbler.

Float a couple of centimetres of red wine on top by pouring it down a spiral-handled bar spoon. Add two straws.

NEW PORT SOUR

THIS MORE PUNCHY VERSION OF A NEW YORK SOUR, THE ADDED KICK COMING FROM THE PORT, PRESENTS MORE OF A CHALLENGE TO THOSE WISHING TO KEEP THE TWO LAYERS DISTINCT — IT IS ALMOST IMPOSSIBLE, BUT THEN SO LONG AS ONE HAS WILLING DRINKERS THERE SHOULD BE NO WASTAGE!

SERVES 1

bourbon	35ml
lemon juice	35ml
Sugar Syrup *(see page 56)*	a dash
Angostura bitters	a dash
late-bottled vintage (LBV) port	50ml

Shake everything except the port in a Boston shaker with ice, then strain over ice in a tumbler.

Float a couple of centimetres of the port on top by pouring it down a spiral-handled bar spoon. Add two straws.

SOHO SOUR

THIS COCKTAIL STARTED THE TREND OF NAMING COCKTAILS TOPOGRAPHICALLY AND BEGAN LIFE AS ONE OF OUR FAVOURITE DRINKS, THE AMARETTO SOUR (50ML AMARETTO, 50ML LEMON JUICE, A DASH OF EGG WHITE, A DASH OF ANGOSTURA BITTERS), FROM WHICH WE REMOVED THE EGG WHITE AND SUBSTITUTED BOURBON. AS THE RATIO OF AMARETTO HAS BEEN REDUCED TO ACCOMMODATE THE BOURBON, SOME SUGAR SYRUP IS NEEDED, BUT YOU NEED TO BE CAREFUL WITH THE QUANTITY TO AVOID MAKING IT OVERLY SWEET. HOWEVER, WITH A LITTLE EXPERIMENTATION IT ISN'T HARD TO MAINTAIN A BALANCE WITH THE SOURNESS OF THE LEMON JUICE.

SERVES 1

bourbon	50ml
amaretto	25ml
lemon juice	25ml
Sugar Syrup *(see page 56)*	a dash
Angostura bitters	a dash

GARNISH

maraschino or bourbon-soaked chery

Shake all the ingredients in a Boston shaker with ice, then strain over ice in a tumbler.

Garnish with a maraschino or bourbon-soaked cherry, and add two straws.

CIDER SOUR

WE ARE VERY LUCKY TO HAVE ACCESS TO THE MOST DELICIOUS FARMHOUSE CIDER, FROM CORNISH ORCHARDS, AND IT SEEMED ONLY LOGICAL TO INCORPORATE IT INTO A COCKTAIL AS WELL. FRAN CAME UP WITH THIS WONDERFUL CONCOCTION, PAIRING IT WITH OUR HOUSE BOURBON. THE SWEETNESS COMES NOT ONLY FROM THE CIDER BUT ALSO FROM OUR OWN GINGER SYRUP, WHICH IS EASILY MADE AND KEEPS VERY WELL. THE RESULT IS A VERY REFRESHING DRINK THAT QUICKLY FOUND ITS WAY TO A PERMANENT PLACE ON OUR COCKTAIL MENU.

SERVES 1

bourbon	35ml
still cider	35ml
lemon juice	25ml
Ginger Syrup *(see page 56)*	25ml

GARNISH

green apple slice

Shake all the ingredients in a Boston shaker with ice, then strain over ice in a tumbler.

Garnish with a slice of green apple, and add two straws.

THE GANTON

PARTLY INSPIRED BY THE SIDE TRUCK AND INFLUENCED BY SOURS, THE GANTON TAKES ITS NAME FROM THE STREET ON THE CORNER WHERE PITT CUE IS LOCATED IN SOHO. WE TRIED TO DO SOME RESEARCH TO DISCOVER THE PROVENANCE OF THE NAME, BUT AS FAR AS WE CAN TELL THE REFERENCE IS TO A TOWN IN NORTH YORKSHIRE WITH A FAMOUS GOLF COURSE.

SERVES 1

rye whiskey	50ml
Cointreau	25ml
lemon juice	25ml
free-range egg white	¼
orange bitters	a dash

GARNISH

orange slice

Shake all the ingredients hard in a Boston shaker with ice, then strain over ice in a tumbler.

Garnish with a slice of orange, and add two straws.

BUZZ CUT

THIS COCKTAIL USES WHITE DOG MASH WHICH IS SOMETHING THAT HAS ONLY RECENTLY COME ON TO THE MARKET, ALTHOUGH IT HAS BEEN AVAILABLE FOR CENTURIES. IT IS THE RAW SPIRIT THAT COMES OFF A STILL BEFORE IT IS PLACED INTO A CHARRED OAK BARREL FOR AGEING — IN EFFECT IT IS MOONSHINE. DESPITE ITS STRENGTH (THE ABV IS SOMEWHERE IN THE REGION OF 63.5%) IT HAS A NOTICEABLE CORN FLAVOUR AND WE KEEP IT ON THE BACK BAR MAINLY AS A CONVERSATION PIECE FOR JAMIE TO START A DISCUSSION ON THE MANUFACTURE OF BOURBON. THIS COCKTAIL WAS NAMED AFTER COLIN GRANDFIELD ON THE OCCASION OF A RATHER DRASTIC HAIRCUT, FOR WHICH REASON IT IS ALSO SERVED WITHOUT A GARNISH.

SERVES 1

applejack (American apple brandy)	50ml
White Dog Mash	12.5ml
lemon juice	25ml
Sugar Syrup (see page 56)	a dash
free-range egg white	¼

Shake all the ingredients hard in a Boston shaker with ice, then strain over ice in a tumbler. No garnish, but add two straws.

FRENCH TOAST

BOURBON OBVIOUSLY, BUT THIS COCKTAIL ALSO RELIES ON CHAMBORD, A FRENCH BLACK RASPBERRY LIQUEUR THAT COMES IN THE MOST HILARIOUS BOTTLE, PACKAGED LIKE AN ORB AND SAID TO DATE BACK TO THE DAYS OF LOUIS XIV.

TO MAKE THIS DRINK, YOU MUST USE PROPER CLOUDY APPLE JUICE, THE NICER THE BETTER; THE CLEAR STUFF JUST WON'T DO. IT IS A DRINK THAT WE OFTEN GIVE TO THOSE WHO CLAIM NOT TO LIKE DRINKS MADE WITH BOURBON … AND IT HAS NEVER FAILED YET.

SERVES 1

bourbon	50ml
Chambord	25ml
apple juice	25ml
cherry bitters	a dash

GARNISH

apple slice

Shake all the ingredients in a Boston shaker with ice, then strain over ice in a tumbler.

Garnish with a slice of apple, and add two straws.

INDIAN SUMMER

THIS IS ONE THAT WE MAKE FOR CUSTOMERS WHO CLAIM NOT TO LIKE WHISKEY.

SERVES 1

rye whiskey	35ml
Cointreau	25ml
lemon juice	20ml
Sugar Syrup (see page 56)	a dash
ginger ale	50ml

GARNISH

thin cucumber slices	3

Shake the whiskey, Cointreau, lemon juice and sugar syrup in a Boston shaker with ice, then strain over ice in a tumbler. Top up the glass with the ginger ale.

Garnish with the thin slices of cucumber, and add two straws.

MAPPLE

THIS DRINK COMBINES JAMIE'S MEMORIES FROM ALL OVER AMERICA: THE MAPLE SYRUP CONJURES UP NEW ENGLAND, THE BOURBON THE SOUTHERN STATES AND THE ORANGE FLORIDA, WHERE HIS GRANDPARENTS LIVED WHEN HE WAS GROWING UP. THE COMBINATION IS AUTUMNAL, BUT DON'T LET IT BE LIMITED TO SERVING AT THAT TIME OF THE YEAR.

SERVES 1

bourbon	25ml
applejack (American apple brandy)	35ml
still cider	25ml
maple syrup	12.5ml
orange bitters	a dash
orange wedge	1

GARNISH

orange slice

Add all the liquid ingredients with ice to a Boston shaker, squeeze over the orange wedge and drop in the wedge as well. Shake, then strain over ice in a tumbler.

Garnish with a slice of orange, and add two straws.

THE SIDE TRUCK

THIS COCKTAIL IS INCLUDED ON OUR MENU IN HOMAGE TO THE SIDECAR, WHICH FAMILY LEGEND HAS IT WAS INVENTED BY JAMIE'S MOTHER'S GODFATHER, WHO WAS AN AIDE TO GENERAL 'BLACK JACK' PERSHING DURING THE FIRST WORLD WAR AND SPENT MOST OF THE WAR IN A MOTORCYCLE SIDECAR NEVER FAR FROM HIS TRUSTY COCKTAIL SHAKER. IN ADAPTING IT FOR PITT CUE, WE REPLACED THE BRANDY WITH BOURBON, AND ADDED SOME BITTERS AND SUGAR SYRUP TO ROUND OFF THE FLAVOURS.

SERVES 1

bourbon	35ml
Cointreau	25ml
lemon juice	25ml
orange bitters	a dash
Sugar Syrup (see page 56)	a dash

GARNISH

orange slice

Shake all the ingredients in a Boston shaker with ice, and strain over ice in a tumbler.

Garnish with a slice of orange, and add two straws.

3 CAMPARI-BASED COCKTAILS

THIS COLLECTION IS ROOTED IN JAMIE'S LOVE OF CAMPARI AND ALL THINGS BITTER.

CAMP AMERICA

THIS COCKTAIL CAME ABOUT AS A RESULT OF BEING PRESENTED WITH A QUANTITY OF BITTER SEVILLE MARMALADE, AND HAS THE ADDED BONUS OF GENERATING CONFUSED LOOKS ON FACES WHEN WE SPOON JAM INTO A COCKTAIL SHAKER. THE TRICK HERE IS TO SHAKE IT WELL TO RELEASE ALL THE DELICIOUS FLAVOUR FROM THE THICK-CUT SEVILLE ORANGE RINDS, THEN STRAIN IT SO THAT NONE OF THE RIND GETS INTO THE GLASS. THE LEMON JUICE BALANCES THE SWEETNESS AND LENDS A WONDERFUL COLOUR TO THE FINISHED DRINK.

SERVES 1

bourbon	50ml
Campari	25ml
thick-cut bitter seville marmalade	2 tsp
lemon juice	a dash

GARNISH

orange or blood orange slice

Shake all the ingredients hard in a Boston shaker with ice, then strain over ice in a tumbler. Garnish with a slice of blood orange, and add two straws.

BOURBORONI

THIS IS A RIFF ON THE NEGRONI, REPLACING THE GIN WITH BOURBON; ITS ACTUAL NAME IS THE BOULEVARDIER, BUT WE THINK THAT BOURBORONI IS MORE FUN AND CERTAINLY GIVES A GREATER HINT AS TO WHAT'S TO FOLLOW. USE THE BEST RED VERMOUTH YOU CAN FIND — THE MOST DELICIOUS WE'VE EVER TRIED IS THE CARPANO ANTICA FORMULA, THE COST OF WHICH WE PRETEND TO JUSTIFY AS IT COMES IN LITRE BOTTLES.

SERVES 1

Campari	35ml
bourbon	35ml
sweet vermouth	35ml

GARNISH

orange slice

Assemble all the ingredients in an ice-filled tumbler and stir to ensure that they are mixed and chilled. Garnish with a slice of orange, no straws.

LBC

THIS COCKTAIL STARTED LIFE AS A
STAFF DRINK — IT WAS SERVED IN RED
SOLO PARTY CUPS THAT WE HAD SHIPPED
FROM AMERICA. THE FIRST LBC WE EVER
SOLD WAS TO A YOUNG WOMAN WHO, WHEN
ASKED WHAT SHE WANTED TO DRINK,
SPOKE OF HER LOVE OF CAMPARI.
IT IS LIGHT AND REFRESHING; ANOTHER
PERFECT SUMMER DRINK.

SERVES 1

bourbon	50ml
Campari	25ml
lemon juice	12.5ml
lime, quartered	1

GARNISH

lime slice

Add all the liquid ingredients with ice to
a Boston shaker, then squeeze over the lime
quarters and drop the limes in as well.
Shake, then strain over ice in a tumbler.

Garnish with a slice of lime, and add
two straws.

HARD LEMONADE I

THIS WAS THE BEST-SELLING DRINK AT
THE PITT CUE TRAILER IN SUMMER.
AT THE RESTAURANT, THE HARD LEMONADE
EVOLVED INTO THE HARD LEMONADE II
(SEE NEXT RECIPE).

SERVES 1

gin	50ml
elderflower cordial	a dash
homemade lemonade, to top up *(see below)*	

GARNISH

lemon slices

Assemble all the ingredients in an
ice-filled tumbler and stir to ensure that
they are mixed and chilled. Garnish with
slices of lemon, and add a straw.

HARD LEMONADE II

THIS IS A PUNCHIER DRINK THAN
ITS ELDER COUSIN, WITH A GREATER
RICHNESS AND COMPLEXITY ACHIEVED
BY REPLACING GIN WITH BOURBON
AND COINTREAU.

SERVES 1

bourbon	35ml
Cointreau	25ml
homemade lemonade, to top up *(see below)*	

GARNISH

lemon slices

Assemble all the ingredients in an
ice-filled tumbler and stir to ensure that
they are mixed and chilled. Garnish with
slices of lemon, and add a straw.

LEMONADE SYRUP

MAKES 400ML

unwaxed lemons	10
sugar (we use soft light brown)	400g
water	350ml

Zest the lemons, then juice them, placing
all the zest and juice in a pan. Add the
sugar and the water and heat slowly,
stirring all the time, until the sugar
has dissolved. The liquid should approach
boiling point, but not boil.

Pass the liquid through a sieve to strain
off the zest and lemon pips.

Bottle while still warm, in sterilized
bottles (see page 78). The syrup can be
kept in the fridge for several weeks.

For homemade lemonade, dilute to taste:
3 or 4 parts water to 1 part syrup.

For a more unusual syrup, you can also try
adding a tiny amount of fresh chilli.

MEAN SHANDY

THE NAME IS A NOD NOT ONLY TO THE MEANTIME BREWERY, WHICH PRODUCED THE DRAUGHT BEER THAT THIS COCKTAIL WAS FIRST MADE WITH, BUT ALSO TO THE FACT THAT, WITH THE ADDITION OF BOURBON, IT IS FAR STRONGER AND TOUGHER THAN THE AVERAGE LAGER SHANDY WE ARE ALL FAMILIAR WITH. SHAKING CARBONATED LIQUIDS IN ANY QUANTITY PRESENTS POSSIBLE HAZARDS, SO MAKE SURE THE SHAKER IS TIGHTLY SEALED AND OPEN IT CAREFULLY ONCE SHAKEN.

SERVES 1

bourbon	50ml
Lemonade Syrup *(see page 42)*	25ml
bottled beer	40ml

GARNISH

lemon slice

Shake all the ingredients in a Boston shaker with ice, then strain over ice in a tumbler. Garnish with a slice of lemon, and add two straws.

KENTUCKY LIBRE

THIS IS OUR VERSION OF THE CLASSIC RUM AND COKE DRINK, THE CUBA LIBRE — SPANISH FOR 'FREE CUBA'. AGAIN THE ORIGINS OF THE NAME ARE UNCERTAIN, BUT ONE THEORY DATES IT BACK TO THE SPANISH-AMERICAN WAR OF 1898, AND THIS IS THE ONE THAT APPEALS TO JAMIE, AS HIS GREAT-GRANDFATHER, ROBERT H. BECKHAM, FOUGHT IN THAT WAR, TAKING PART IN THE FAMOUS ACTION ON SAN JUAN HILL.

SERVES 1

bourbon	50ml
homemade cola, to top up *(see page 56)*	

GARNISH

lime wedge

Assemble all the ingredients in an ice-filled tumbler and stir to ensure that they are mixed and chilled.

Garnish with a wedge of lime, and add one long straw.

CHERRY COLA

ANOTHER COLA-BASED COCKTAIL, THE CHERRY COLA SELLS INCREDIBLY WELL, BUT THEN AGAIN THE DELICIOUS COMBINATION OF CHERRY AND COLA HAS LONG BEEN UNDERSTOOD. THIS COCKTAIL INSPIRED A SIMPLER VERSION THAT WE SERVE ON THE TRAILER — THE TRASH (SEE RECIPE BELOW).

SERVES 1

bourbon	50ml
Cherry Heering	25ml
lemon juice	25ml
Cola Syrup *(see page 56)*	20ml

GARNISH

maraschino cherry

Shake all the ingredients in a Boston shaker with ice, then strain over ice in a tumbler.

Garnish with a maraschino cherry, and add two straws.

TRASH

OUR CREATION HERE IS TRYING TO MATCH THE FLAVOUR PROFILE OF THAT STABLE OF THE 1980S, CHERRY COKE - THE FIRST OF THAT RATHER DUBIOUS FAMILY OF 'FLAVOURED COKES' TO SEE THE LIGHT OF DAY. WE WANTED SOMETHING BOOZY YET DECADENT; THAT WOULD TASTE SLIGHTLY 'WRONG' AS IT WERE, BUT IN A CHEERFUL WAY.

SERVES 1

bourbon	35ml
Cherry Heering	25ml
cherry bitters	a dash
cola, to top up	

GARNISH

maraschino cherry

Add all the ingredients to a tall glass and stir well.

Garnish with a maraschino cherry, and add two straws.

BOOM TOWN

THIS COCKTAIL USES OUR OWN COLA SYRUP, UNLIKE THE FORMULA FOR COCA COLA, WHICH SINCE ITS CREATION IN 1886 HAS BEEN JEALOUSLY GUARDED, OURS IS AVAILABLE ON PAGE 56. LIME JUICE IS USED TO CUT THROUGH THE SWEETNESS OF THE COLA SYRUP, AND WE RECOMMEND PLACING THE SQUEEZED WEDGES IN THE SHAKER AND SHAKING THEM TOGETHER WITH THE LIQUID TO INCREASE THE INTENSITY OF THE FLAVOUR, AS MORE WILL BE EXTRACTED FROM THE RIND DURING THE SHAKING PROCESS.

SERVES 1

bourbon	35ml
Cola Syrup (see page 56)	35ml
draught beer	35ml
lime wedges, squeezed	4

GARNISH

lime wedge

Shake all the ingredients including the squeezed lime wedges in a Boston shaker with ice, then strain over ice in a tumbler.

Garnish with a wedge of lime, and add one long straw.

PITT PONY

THIS DRINK WENT THROUGH A COUPLE OF NAME CHANGES: IT STARTED OUT AS A KENTUCKY MULE, IN RECOGNITION OF ITS DEBT TO THE MOSCOW MULE, BUT NOONE ORDERED IT WHEN IT FIRST WENT ON THE SPECIALS BOARD, SO THE PITT PONY WAS BORN. IT IS OF COURSE POSSIBLE TO USE SHOP-BOUGHT GINGER BEER (THOUGH IT ISN'T QUITE AS MUCH FUN AS MAKING YOUR OWN) BUT IN THAT CASE THE RESULT WILL BE MUCH SWEETER.

SERVES 1

lime wedges	3
bourbon	50ml
Angostura bitters	a dash
ginger beer (preferably homemade), to top up	

Squeeze the lime wedges into a half-pint glass and drop in the squeezed wedges as well. Then pour over the bourbon and add the bitters before stirring the whole mixture together with ginger beer.

Garnish with the squeezed lime wedges, and add one long straw.

HAIR OF THE HOG

BACON VODKA IS DEVILISHLY EASY TO MAKE. SIMPLY FRY SOME SMOKED STREAKY BACON IN A PAN UNTIL CRISPY, THEN DEGLAZE THE PAN WITH SOME VODKA. PLACE THE BACON, ALL THE JUICES AND THE REST OF THE VODKA IN A SEALED CONTAINER TO STEEP, THEN FREEZE IT BEFORE STRAINING THE CONTENTS TO PRODUCE BACON VODKA. THE CHEAPER THE BACON, THE MORE INTENSE THE VODKA. THE SPICIER THE DRINK, THE BETTER IN OUR OPINION, BUT MAKE SURE THERE AREN'T TOO MANY BITS IN THE SPICE MIX, AS THEY ALL END UP AT THE BOTTOM OF YOUR GLASS.

SERVES 1

bacon-infused vodka	50ml
tomato juice	75ml
Spice Mix *(see page 57)*	1 tsp (or to taste)

Assemble all the ingredients over ice in a shaker, stir, then strain into a tumbler, no ice.

Add two straws and serve with Fennel Cured Scratchings (see page 62).

PINK PIG

IF YOU'VE MADE IT THIS FAR LOOKING FOR A COCKTAIL WITHOUT BOURBON IN IT AND NOT BEEN IMPRESSED WITH THE TWO ALREADY ON OFFER, LET US INTRODUCE THE PINK PIG: MADE WITH RHUBARB SYRUP, OR AT LEAST THE LIQUOR LEFT OVER WHEN STEWING RHUBARB, IT IS ALSO A SEASONAL COCKTAIL — LIGHT AND REFRESHING, THE LEMON MAKES SURE THERE IS SOME RESIDUAL TARTNESS.

SERVES 1

gin	50ml
rhubarb syrup	25ml
lemon juice	a dash
Sugar Syrup *(see page 56)*	a dash

GARNISH

lemon slice

Shake all the ingredients in a Boston shaker with ice, then strain over ice in a tumbler.

Garnish with a slice of lemon, and add two straws.

BOURBON HOT TODDY

THIS TODDY IS PERFECT FOR A COLD DAY, AND WHILE ITS CURATIVE POWERS IN DEALING WITH A COLD MAY BE IN DOUBT MEDICALLY, THERE IS LITTLE DOUBT THAT PSYCHOLOGICALLY THE PATIENT IS BETTER OFF FOR DRINKING ONE. PLACE THE CLOVE-STUDDED LEMON SLICE IN THE BOTTOM OF THE GLASS AND ADD SOME OF THE BOILING WATER IMMEDIATELY TO RELEASE NOT ONLY THE FLAVOUR OF THE LEMON BUT ALSO THE INTENSITY OF THE CLOVE ESSENCE. THE OVERALL EFFECT SURE TAKES THE STING OUT OF BEING LAID UP WITH THE FLU.

SERVES 1

bourbon	50ml
lemon juice	25ml
Honey Syrup *(see page 56)*	a dash
Ginger Syrup *(see page 56)*	a dash
orange bitters	a dash
boiling water, to top up	

GARNISH

lemon slice, studded with cloves

Asssemble all the ingredients in a half-pint glass and stir. Garnish with a lemon slice studded with cloves, no straw.

GODFATHER

WHILE ON THE SUBJECT OF GODFATHERS, THIS SEEMS A GOOD PLACE TO PUT THIS COCKTAIL, WHICH JAMIE MADE SURE WAS ON THE MENU AT HIS GODSON JACKSON BOXER'S BAR, AT BRUNSWICK HOUSE, AND THAT MAKES OCCASIONAL APPEARANCES AS A SPECIAL COCKTAIL AT PITT CUE. THOUGH SURPRISINGLY DRINKABLE, THE LACK OF ANY MIXER MAKES IT NOT FOR THE FAINT-HEARTED; THE BITTERS BALANCE THE SWEETNESS OF THE AMARETTO.

SERVES 1

bourbon	50ml
amaretto	35ml
orange bitters	a dash

GARNISH

orange slice

Assemble all the ingredients in an ice-filled tumbler and stir to ensure that they are mixed and chilled.

Garnish with a slice of orange, and add two straws.

GODFATHER PART II

RUNNING WITH THE GODFATHER THEME, HERE THE AMARETTO IS REPLACED BY TUACA, AN ITALIAN VANILLA AND CITRUS LIQUEUR.

SERVES 1

bourbon	50ml
Tuaca	35ml
chocolate bitters	a dash

GARNISH

candied orange zest

Assemble all the ingredients in an ice-filled tumbler and stir to ensure that they are mixed and chilled.

Garnish with a piece of candied orange zest, and add two straws.

— SYRUPS —

SYRUPS KEEP FOR UP TO 2 WEEKS OR A MONTH IN THE FRIDGE, AND CAN BE USED FOR COCKTAILS AND OTHER DRINKS SUCH AS COFFEE AND ICED TEA.

SUGAR SYRUP

MAKES APPROXIMATELY 750ML

boiling water	500ml
caster sugar	500g

Pour freshly boiling water on to the sugar and stir until it dissolves.

Leave to cool, then pour into sterilized bottles (see page 78) and store in the fridge for up to a month.

GINGER SYRUP

MAKES APPROXIMATELY 375ML

boiling water	200ml
caster sugar	150g
fresh root ginger, peeled and finely grated (preferably Microplaned)	150g

Pour freshly boiling water on to the sugar and ginger and gently stir until the sugar dissolves.

Allow to steep, then strain and pour into sterilized bottles (see page 78). Store in the fridge for up to a month.

Dilute to taste: about 3 or 4 parts water to 1 part syrup.

COLA SYRUP

MAKES APPROXIMATELY 300ML

water	200ml
caster sugar	250g
zest of 1 lime, 1 lemon and ½ an orange	
star anise	1
ground ginger	½ tsp
ground cinnamon	½ tsp
grated nutmeg	a pinch
demerara sugar	1 tbsp

Pour the water into a pan and add the caster sugar, citrus zests and spices. Simmer over a low heat for 1 hour, then strain through a sieve lined with two clean J Cloths.

Add the demerara sugar, stirring until it dissolves — this adds colour to the syrup. Dilute to taste: about 3 or 4 parts water to 1 part syrup. Store in sterilized bottles in the fridge for up to 2 weeks.

HONEY SYRUP

MAKES APPROXIMATELY 375ML

boiling water	200ml
honey	175ml

Pour the boiling water on to the honey and stir until the honey has dissolved. Store in sterilized bottles in the fridge for up to 2 weeks.

SPICE MIX

MAKES APPROXIMATELY 750ML

BASE

lemon juice	275ml
cider vinegar	175ml
Worcestershire sauce	200ml

SPICES

chilli flakes	25g
cayenne pepper	15g
paprika	15g
dried celery	15g
fennel seeds	15g

freshly ground black pepper	10g
garlic powder	5g
ground cumin	5g
paprika	5g
brown sugar	25g
salt	5g

Mix the base ingredients together and stir in the spices, sugar and salt. Allow to steep overnight, then strain to yield a devilishly spicy hot sauce. Use in Hair of the Hog (see page 50) and other restorative drinks. It should keep for a week stored in a sealed container in the icebox.

CHAPTER

SNACKS

SNACKS

· · · · · · · · · · · ·

During the first summer of trading from the trailer we came up close and personal with the realities of cooking outdoors in a British summer. When summer did show its face there were few things more pleasant, and late balmy evenings by the Thames often became debauched bourbon- and barbecue-fuelled parties that went long into the night and the following morning. However, when the summer sun was not so willing, the grey and wet afternoons were all about snacking, occasionally a 'mystery cocktail hour' or a nap on the floor by the oven, and constant development in the search for the perfect 'scooby snack' to keep any boredom at bay. It was, in fact, a disguised blessing that it rained most of the time, with bourbon intake and partying largely relative to sunny hours by the river, and by the start of September when we closed the trailer for the summer our new waistlines were testament to all the rainy days spent gorging on the fruits of our snacky pursuits.

Our first menus on the trailer were really snack-heavy, based upon what we fancied cooking that day and what we found at the market each morning. Such was our approach to most things when we started the trailer, so over-exuberant and unbelieving were we that we were actually doing our own thing, most snacks (and drinks in fact) were rarely sold on the menu but handed out gratis to whichever customers seemed most willing to try them.

While we did not exactly run the trailer like the well-oiled machine the accountant might have hoped, giving away, eating and drinking as much bourbon, beer and food as we sold, it was such an exciting time to cook and provided the blueprint for the restaurant and its menu. Those early days in the trailer really began our love affair with good snacking and proved their worth. With an onsetting panic hunger, whether standing at the bar having a drink or sitting at the table waiting for the main event to arrive or even just well-oiled, there are very few times when a solid snack will not be welcome and steadying. These trials and errors in the trailer unsurprisingly led to the restaurant menu having its own designated 'snack' section for whatever we are in the mood to serve. With this section playing such a fundamental role in the restaurant, it seems only right to dedicate a little part of this book to a few of those snacks that have the ability to fill a hole when it most needs filling.

We have, unfortunately, had to leave out a great number of those snacks that have featured on the menu at various times, and also those which have never been on an actual printed menu but were made and served nonetheless when we opened the trailer.

· · · · · · · · · · · ·

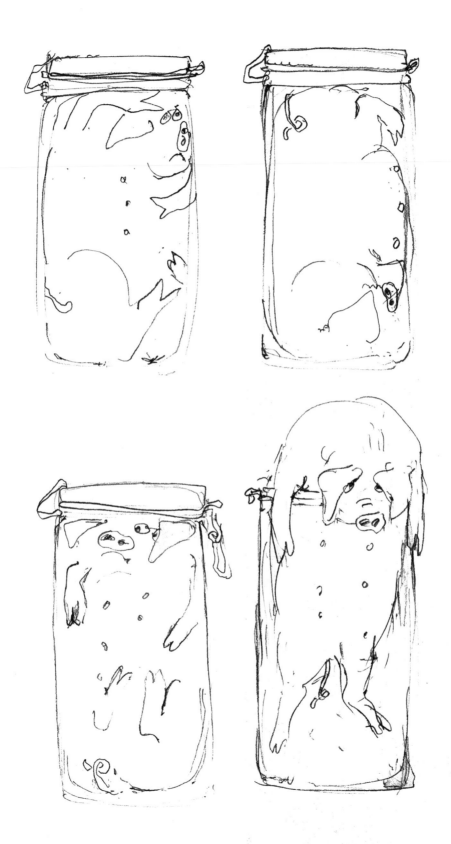

FENNEL CURED
SCRATCHINGS

THIS RECIPE WAS BORN FROM THE LIMITATIONS OF OUR SOHO KITCHEN.
WHEN THE TRAILER FIRST OPENED WE HAD ACCESS TO A PIZZA OVEN THAT
WAS BRILLIANT FOR MAKING CRISPY PIGS' SKIN, BUT IN THE SMALL HOBBIT DEN
IN SOHO WE HAVE NO SUCH LUXURY. SO, ALTHOUGH IT MAY SEEM A TOUCH
LABORIOUS TO BE CURING, ROLLING, POACHING AND FRYING SKIN, ALL THIS
LABOUR IS REWARDED WITH THESE VERY TASTY BITS OF CRISPY PIG.

WE DO NOT WASH THE SKINS AFTER CURING, PREFERRING A SCRATCHING THAT IS FULLY
SEASONED OUT OF THE FRYER AND COATED IN HOT AROMATS. A PERFECT BEER BUDDY.

SERVES 4

pork skin, from a whole skinned	
pork neck end *(see page 135)*	250g
Dry Cure *(see page 119)*, made without	
the molasses sugar	15g
oil, for deep-frying	

Sprinkle both sides of the skin with the dry
cure, then roll up the skin into a sausage
(like an Arctic roll) so that the fat side
remains on the inside. Place the sausage
on a long length of clingfilm and roll it up
very tightly. Tie off each end so that the
roll is watertight and leave in the fridge
for at least 24 hours.

Bring a medium pan of water to a gentle
simmer and add the roll of skin. Weight
it down with a heatproof plate and simmer
over a low heat for 1 hour, until the roll
is squidgy and soft to touch. Remove from
the pan and leave to cool, then refrigerate
until you are ready to cook.

Unwrap the skin from the clingfilm and slice
the roll of skin into 5mm rings. Heat the oil
to 180°C in a deep-fat fryer or large saucepan
and fry the rings for 4-5 minutes, or until
golden and crispy. The scratchings should
not need seasoning.

—— HABANERO PIGS' EARS ——

CRISPY PIGS' EARS FIRST MADE AN APPEARANCE IN THE RESTAURANT AS A SIMPLE ACCESSORY FOR OUR SMOKED PIG'S HEAD. THE EARS DEVELOP A LEATHERY QUALITY WHEN SMOKED FOR A LONG PERIOD OF TIME, SO THEY ARE REMOVED WHEN SMOKING THE HEADS. THIS GIVES US THE EARS TO PLAY AROUND WITH AND THERE IS NO DOUBT THEY ARE BEST WHEN CRISPY. IT IS WORTH NOTING THAT NOT ALL PIGS HAVE EARS THAT ARE BEST MEANT FOR THE POT. OUR MIDDLE WHITE PIGS ON THE FARM IN PITT, FOR INSTANCE, HAVE SMALL BAT-LIKE EARS THAT ARE DELICIOUS, BUT WHEN COMPARED TO A GLOUCESTER OLD SPOT, CORNISH LOP OR LARGE BLACK, WHICH ARE ALL BLESSED WITH EARS THAT COVER MOST OF THEIR FACE, THEY SEEM SLIGHTLY LESS POT-WORTHY.

SERVES 2

large pigs' ears, shaved, and ready for cooking	4
peeled and finely chopped vegetables (onion, carrot, celery, leek, garlic)	100g
black peppercorns	10
faggot of herbs (thyme, rosemary, bay, 3 dried chillies)	1
oil, for deep-frying	
Habanero Rub *(see below)*, to taste	

HABANERO RUB

granulated sugar	20g
Maldon sea salt	40g
fennel seeds, toasted	10g
coriander seeds, toasted	10g
chilli flakes	1 tsp
dried habanero chillies	1 tsp
black peppercorns	5g
finely grated zest of 1 lime	

Put all the ingredients for the habanero rub into a blender and blitz to a rough powder. Place in an airtight container until needed.

Fill a medium saucepan with cold water, add the pigs' ears and bring to the boil. Drain, discarding the water, then fill the pan with fresh cold water. Add the vegetables, peppercorns and the faggot of herbs. Bring to a low simmer and cook the pigs' ears for 1½–2 hours, or until gelatinous and giving, continually skimming the surface of the pan and making sure the liquid never boils. Carefully remove the ears to a tray and refrigerate overnight until firm and dry.

The next day, heat the oil to 180°C in a deep-fryer or large saucepan.

Slice the ears into long thin strips (they should be roughly 8cm long and 5mm wide). Then, working in small batches, drop the strips into the fryer. If you add too many at once they will stick together and you will get a misshapen 'ear cake', by no means a hardship to eat, but not what we are looking for. Check after 3–4 minutes — the strips should be golden and crisp.

Remove them from the fryer on to kitchen paper and season with a liberal shaking of the habanero rub. Serve with a helping of either Kimchi (see page 214), Nduja Mayonnaise (see page 232) or aioli, and definitely a cold beer.

— CRUMBED PIGS' CHEEKS —

PIGS' CHEEKS ARE ONE OF THE BEST PARTS OF THE ANIMAL. AS A MUSCLE THEY
HAVE BEEN WELL-WORKED, DUE TO THOSE LITTLE CHAPS CONSTANTLY EATING,
AND CONTAIN LOTS OF COLLAGEN THAT MELTS INTO BEAUTIFULLY GELATINOUS
LOVELINESS! THIS JUST MEANS THEY NEED TO BE COOKED FOR LONGER TO BREAK
THE MUSCLES RIGHT DOWN. THIS IS A REALLY SIMPLE RECIPE WHICH PRODUCES
A SUPER EPIC SNACK. IN THE RESTAURANT WE USE THE CHEEK MUSCLE ITSELF,
ABOUT THE SIZE OF A FLATTENED GOLF BALL IF SUCH A THING EVEN EXISTS.
SERVE THEM WITH SOME APPLE KETCHUP, AND YOU'RE WINNING.

MAKES 10

pigs' cheeks, inner muscle only	10
dark soy sauce	80ml
honey	100g
trotter stock or pork stock	200ml
smoked dripping	100ml
mirin	20ml
star anise	4
plain flour	100g
free-range eggs	4
milk	40ml
Japanese panko breadcrumbs	100g
vegetable oil, for deep-frying	

Heat your oven to 150°C/300°F/gas mark 2.

Heat a large casserole dish on the hob and
drizzle in some oil, add the pigs' cheeks
and lightly brown on both sides. Add the
soy sauce, honey, stock, dripping, mirin and
star anise and bring to a simmer. Cover, and
braise in the oven for about 3 hours, or
until the cheeks are tender and juicy.

Remove the cheeks from the sauce and set
aside to cool. In a separate pan reduce the
cooking liquid over a high heat until it is
a sticky sauce, then remove from the heat
and keep warm.

Time to crumb your cheeks. Get ready three
shallow bowls. In the first put the flour.
In the second, beat the eggs with the milk,
and put the panko breadcrumbs into the
third.

Coat the cheeks first in flour, dusting off
any excess. Next dip into the eggs and milk,
then lastly coat in panko breadcrumbs.

Heat the oil to 190°C in a deep-fat fryer
and fry the cheeks for 1 minute or until
golden. Drain well, then serve with the
reserved cooking sauce on the side and some
Apple Ketchup (see page 126). Very cheeky.

— BUFFALO PIGS' TAILS —

MOST GOOD BUTCHERS WILL BE ABLE TO SOURCE YOU SOME TAILS WITH A BIT OF NOTICE. YOU MAY FEEL SLIGHTLY WEIRD ASKING FOR A BAG OF TAILS — IT IS NOT EXACTLY A STAPLE IN THE WEEKLY GROCERY SHOP — BUT THEY ARE A WORTHY PART OF THE PIG AND SHOULD BE USED FOR MORE THAN JUST A GOOD STOCK. IF THEY ARE A TOUCH HAIRY, FIND A RAZOR AND GIVE THEM A GOOD SHAVE.

THE TAILS NEED TO COME OUT OF THE BRAISING LIQUID VERY TENDER — YOUR FINGERNAIL SHOULD PIERCE THE SKIN WITHOUT ANY EFFORT AFTER BRAISING. TAILS REQUIRE THE SAME HANDS-ON APPROACH AS A CHICKEN WING, AND BENEFIT THOSE PEOPLE PARTIAL TO GNAWING AT THE BONE.

SERVES 4

pigs' tails	4
chicken stock	500ml
Hot Sauce (see page 124)	200ml
unsalted butter	100g
cider vinegar	100ml
plain flour	100g
Pork Rub (see page 118)	60g
free-range eggs	4
milk	30ml
Japanese panko breadcrumbs	200g
oil, for deep-frying	

STILTON SAUCE

soured cream	100g
mayonnaise	100g
Stilton cheese (we use Colston Bassett or Stichelton, which is technically not a Stilton)	120g

Heat your oven to 150°C/300°F/gas mark 2.

Put the tails in a casserole, cover with water and bring to the boil. Once boiled, remove from the heat and drain the tails, discarding the water. Return the tails to the casserole and cover with the chicken stock, then place uncovered in the oven for 6 hours, or overnight, until tender. When cooked, remove the tails from the stock and allow to cool.

To make the Stilton Sauce: put the soured cream and mayonnaise into a blender with 100g of the Stilton and blitz until smooth. Pour into a bowl and crumble over the remaining Stilton. Set aside.

Put the hot sauce, butter and cider vinegar into a pan and warm gently, whisking until emulsified. Keep warm.

Get ready three shallow bowls. In the first, mix the flour with the pork rub. In the second, beat the eggs with the milk, and put the panko breadcrumbs into the third. Lightly coat the tails with flour, then dip them into the egg and milk mixture, and finally roll them gently in the panko breadcrumbs. Heat the oil to 180°C in a deep-fat fryer and deep-fry the tails for 2–3 minutes, or until golden and crispy.

Dip the crispy pigs' tails into the warm sauce and serve with the Stilton Sauce and Pickled Celery (see page 194).

OXTAIL & OGLESHIELD NUGGETS

THE CHICKEN NUGGET WAS INVENTED, BELIEVE IT OR NOT, BY A PROFESSOR AT CORNELL UNIVERSITY IN THE 1950S, INTENT, AS ONE IS, ON REFORMING CHICKEN INTO A VARIETY OF UNNATURAL SHAPES. HE DID THIS THROUGH THE RATHER UNSAVOURY CREATION OF 'MEAT SLURRY' OR 'MALLEABLE MEAT', WHEREBY MEAT AND MUSCLES ARE BROKEN DOWN AND EMULSIFIED TO FACILITATE RESHAPING INTO SOMETHING SMALL, BONELESS, AND UNNATURAL. IT HAS ALWAYS BAFFLED US AS TO WHY PEOPLE WOULD TAKE A CHICKEN, BLITZ, PURÉE, CRUSH AND RECONSTITUTE IT BACK INTO THE SAME DRUMSTICK FORM FROM WHENCE IT CAME. PEOPLE CANNOT BE THAT AFRAID OF BONES, SURELY? BUT, THE PROFESSOR AT CORNELL GOES UNDER THE RADAR, FOR IT WAS FAST FOOD THAT GAVE THE NUGGET CENTRE STAGE AND IS RESPONSIBLE FOR OUR GUILTY APPRECIATION OF THE EMULSIFIED 'CHICKEN' NUGGET. WE, OF COURSE, AVOID THE RECONSTITUTED CHICKEN ROUTE AND INSTEAD MANIFEST OUR LOVE OF A MEATY BITE-SIZED SNACK IN OXTAIL FORM. THE PICKED MEAT, PACKED FULL OF GELATINE, LENDS ITSELF VERY WELL TO BECOMING A NUGGET, AND THE CHUNKS OF CHEESE DOTTED THROUGHOUT ARE A GOOEY NO-BRAINER.

IF YOU CANNOT FIND THE WONDERFUL OGLESHIELD CHEESE OR CHEDDAR CHEESE CURDS, THEN A SWISS RACLETTE-STYLE CHEESE OR DECENT CHEDDAR WILL SUFFICE.

SERVES 4

oxtail, chopped into 1-bone sections	1kg
House Rub (see page 119)	125g
Mother Sauce (see page 120)	80ml
Ogleshield cheese or Cheddar cheese curds, cut into 1cm dice	100g
Japanese panko breadcrumbs	100g
plain flour, sifted	100g
free-range eggs	5
oil, for deep-frying	
Maldon sea salt	
freshly ground black pepper	

Prepare a barbecue for smoking (see The Set-Up on pages 114–15) and set the temperature to 110°C.

Coat the oxtail evenly with 100g of the house rub. Shake off any excess. Put the oxtail on the barbecue and smoke for 8 hours, or until the meat pulls away from the bones with little effort. The internal temperature should be around 88°C.

Pick all the oxtail meat from the bones and mix it with the mother sauce, the remaining rub and the diced cheese. Season with salt and pepper to taste. Place the mixture on a long sheet of clingfilm and roll it into a tight sausage about 5cm wide. Tie off the ends and refrigerate to firm up overnight.

Next day, remove the clingfilm and cut the sausage into 1.5cm thick discs. Get ready three shallow bowls. In the first put the sifted flour, in the second beat the eggs, and in the third put the panko breadcrumbs. Lightly coat the nuggets with flour, then dip them into the eggs, and finally roll them gently in the panko breadcrumbs.

Heat the oil to 180°C in a deep-fryer or large saucepan and deep-fry the nuggets in batches for 2 minutes, or until golden. Drain on kitchen paper, then serve with Kimchi Hot Sauce (see page 124).

SMOKED LIVERS

POULTRY OFFAL IS UNDOUBTEDLY THE MOST ACCESSIBLE OF ALL OFFALS AND THE STARTING POINT FOR ANYONE SLIGHTLY SQUEAMISH ABOUT EATING THE 'OTHER BITS' OF THE ANIMAL. LIVERS AND HEARTS ARE INCREDIBLY GOOD VALUE, PERHAPS THE CHEAPEST OF ALL MEAT OFFERINGS AND HAVE THE ABILITY TO BE TRANSFORMED INTO THE MOST DELICIOUS.

THOUGH NOT EASY TO FIND, THERE ARE A FEW GOOSE FARMERS WHO REMAIN HELL-BENT ON PRODUCING FOIE GRAS JUST AS THOSE GLUTTONOUS ROMANS DID WHEN THEY FIRST DISCOVERED THAT A GOOSE TAKES TO FATTENING AND GORGING ITSELF BEFORE ITS ANNUAL MIGRATION. SUCH FREE-RANGE GEESE LIVE UP TO 9 MONTHS WITHOUT ANY FORCE-FEEDING, UNLIKE MUCH FOIE GRAS THAT HITS THE SHELVES AT A STAGGERING 6 WEEKS OF AGE.

THIS RECIPE IS BASED UPON A CLASSIC PARFAIT WITH THE LIVERS SMOKED FOR JUST A FEW MINUTES BEFORE BEING TREATED AS YOU WOULD IN A NORMAL RECIPE. THE FOIE GRAS REALLY DOES ADD SOMETHING EXTRA SEXY TO THE RECIPE, BUT IT CAN BE REPLACED WITH MORE DUCK LIVERS IF GOOD ETHICAL FOIE GRAS PROVES HARD TO OBTAIN. SIMILARLY, CHICKEN LIVERS MAKE A PERFECTLY LOVELY SUBSTITUTE FOR THE DUCK LIVERS. IF YOUR BUTCHER HAS DUCK HEARTS ON SHOW WHEN YOU BUY YOUR LIVERS, SNATCH THEM UP WITHOUT A THOUGHT, THEN GRILL THEM QUICKLY AND TOP THE TOASTS WITH THEM.

SERVES 4

duck livers	100g
fresh foie gras	100g
small free-range eggs	2
unsalted butter, melted	200g

REDUCTION

bourbon	20ml
maple syrup	20ml
shallots, finely chopped	2
black peppercorns, toasted	½ tsp
fennel seeds, toasted	½ tsp
generous sprig of thyme	1
smoked Maldon sea salt	1 tsp

Prepare a barbecue for smoking (see The Set-Up on pages 114-15) and set the temperature to 90°C.

Put the duck livers and foie gras into a shallow tin or dish and smoke in the barbecue for 5 minutes. Very little smoke is required — too much can quickly overpower the livers.

Meanwhile, heat the oven to 160°C/325°F/ gas mark 3. Put all the ingredients for the reduction into a pan and simmer until reduced by half.

Put the smoked livers into a blender with the warm reduction. Add the eggs and blitz until smooth, then continue to blend while pouring in the melted butter in a slow, steady stream until everything is combined.

Pass the mixture through a fine sieve into 4 ramekins and cover with foil. Stand the ramekins in a roasting tray and pour in water to come halfway up the sides, then bake in the oven for 1 hour. Remove from the oven and leave to cool before refrigerating. Serve with toast and pickles.

SMOKED OX CHEEK
— ON TOAST WITH PICKLED WALNUTS —

OX CHEEKS ARE GREAT FRESHLY SMOKED, BUT WHEN CHILLED THEY SET VERY WELL FOR SLICING, AND BECAUSE THE CHEEK IS SUCH A DENSE MUSCLE, IT PAN-FRIES BEAUTIFULLY. THIS IS VERY GOOD TO KNOW IF, HEAVEN FORBID, YOU HAVE ANY LEFTOVERS FROM YOUR DINNER. THE TOAST ACTS JUST LIKE A TRENCHER IN THIS RECIPE (SEE PAGE 166), ONLY CHEEK-SIZED.

WHILE WE PICKLE ALMOST ANYTHING AND EVERYTHING IN THE RESTAURANT, YOU REALLY CANNOT BEAT A JAR OF OPIES PICKLED WALNUTS.

MAKES 4 SMALL TOASTS

ox cheek	1, weighing about 500g
House Rub (see page 119)	40g
slices of sourdough bread, 1cm thick	4
butter or Whipped Bone Marrow (see page 228), for spreading	
Barbecue Sauce (see page 122)	100ml
pickled walnuts, cut into 5mm slices (we use Opies)	1 jar
fresh horseradish (or use horseradish cream)	1 stick

Prepare a barbecue for smoking (see The Set-Up on pages 114-15) and set the temperature to 110°C.

Rub the ox cheek all over with the house rub, shaking off any excess, and smoke for 7–8 hours. The cheek will shrink and the internal temperature should be about 86–88°C. It should be slightly soft and gelatinous to the touch when cooked, and long tendrils of gelatine may well be hanging from the underside. When ready, remove the cheek, wrap in foil and leave to rest for 10 minutes.

Toast the sourdough well on both sides, then butter or spread with whipped bone marrow on one side. Cut the ox cheek into 1cm slices. Grill or pan-fry the cheek slices over a high heat until caramelized on both sides. Once caramelized, begin to brush with the barbecue sauce.

Top each toast with a slice of cheek, and finish with several slices of pickled walnut and a liberal grating of fresh horseradish.

SMOKED LAMB MARROW
── WITH ANCHOVY ──

LAMB MARROWS HAVE ALL THE UNCTUOUSNESS OF BEEF MARROW BUT WITH LOVELY LAMB FLAVOURS COMING THROUGH — TELL YOUR BUTCHER YOU WANT THE EQUIVALENT OF BEEF MARROW SHAFTS, BUT FROM LAMB.

SHOOTING PICKLE BRINE AFTER EATING THESE IS OPTIONAL, BUT HAS GREAT RESTORATIVE BALANCING POWERS AFTER EATING THE RICH AND FATTY MARROW.

SERVES 4

lamb marrow bones, split	4
smoked anchovy fillets	8
parsley, chopped	10g
shallot, chopped	1
garlic clove, crushed	1
sourdough breadcrumbs	10g
finely grated zest of 1 lemon	
slices of sourdough bread, 1cm thick	8
smoked Maldon sea salt	
freshly ground black pepper	

TO SERVE

4 large shots of chilled pickle juice from Bread & Butter Pickles (see page 191)

Prepare a barbecue for direct grilling (see pages 112–15) and set the temperature to 180°C.

Carefully cut the bone marrow into 5mm dice and put into a bowl. Dice half the anchovies and mix with the parsley, shallot, garlic, breadcrumbs and lemon zest and season with smoked salt and pepper. Carefully combine with the diced bone marrow and put the mixture into the 4 split marrow bones.

Place the marrow bones, filled side up, on the barbecue and grill with the lid closed for 6 minutes. Place on kitchen paper to drain away any excess fat, then arrange on a serving plate.

Lay half a smoked anchovy fillet on top of each bone and serve with toasted sourdough slices. Once consumed, shoot the chilled pickle juice with haste.

SMOKED FOIE GRAS
— ON TOAST WITH PICKLED CHERRIES —

WHILE FORCE-FEEDING IS REQUIRED TO MEET THE FRENCH DEFINITION OF FOIE GRAS, THERE ARE PRODUCERS IN SPAIN AND ITALY THAT DO NOT FORCE-FEED BIRDS IN ORDER TO PRODUCE FATTENED LIVERS, ALLOWING THEM TO EAT FREELY. INTEREST IN ALTERNATIVE PRODUCTION METHODS HAS GROWN, DUE TO ETHICAL CONCERNS, AND SUCH LIVERS ARE CALLED FATTY GOOSE LIVER OR ETHICAL FOIE GRAS. THIS METHOD INVOLVES TIMING THE SLAUGHTER TO COINCIDE WITH THE WINTER MIGRATION, WHEN LIVERS ARE NATURALLY FATTENED.

SERVES 6

fresh foie gras	1 lobe, weighing about 600g
Duck Rub (see page 118)	50g
slices of sourdough bread, 1cm thick	6
Pickled Cherries (see page 197)	12

Prepare a barbecue for smoking (see The Set-Up on pages 114-15). Set the temperature to 180°C and put a small ovenproof pan directly over the coals to heat.

Coat the foie gras with half the duck rub — it should form a crust. Place it in the pan and cook in the barbecue for 5 minutes on each side. It should be well caramelized and slightly soft to touch, and the internal temperature should reach 50°C. Remove the pan from the heat and leave the foie gras to rest for 5 minutes.

Meanwhile, toast the sourdough slices. Cut the foie gras at an angle into 1cm slices and lay them on the toast. Season with more duck rub and eat at once, with the pickled cherries.

OUR PICKLE BRINE

THIS PICKLE BRINE IS A VERY BASIC
PICKLE, A STARTING POINT. MAKE IT, TRY
IT, THEN GO FROM THERE WITH DIFFERENT
AROMATICS, VINEGARS AND SUGARS TO
MAKE MORE INTERESTING PICKLES. THE
BRINE REFRIGERATES WELL, SO IT IS
WORTH MAKING A GOOD AMOUNT IF YOU
PLAN ON DOING A LOT OF PICKLING,
THOUGH YOU CAN EASILY SCALE IT DOWN
SIMPLY BY HALVING THE AMOUNTS.

MAKES 2.5 LITRES

water	1.5 litres
cider vinegar	1 litre
caster or demerara sugar	700g
sea salt	30g

optional aromats (peppercorns, bay leaves,
fennel seeds, coriander seeds, mustard seeds,
star anise, cardamom pods, garlic, root liquorice)

Put all the ingredients into a large pan
and bring to the boil, stirring occasionally
until the sugar and salt are dissolved.

Prepare whatever fruit or vegetables you
want to pickle and drop them into the hot
brine. Leave to cool, then refrigerate in
sterilized jars for 3—5 days.

This pickle works especially well for
carrots, celery, beetroot, fennel bulbs,
cauliflower, kohlrabi, peas and chillies.

· To sterilize jars, thoroughly wash and dry your jars and lids.
Place the jars in a cold oven and heat to 160°C/325°F/
gas mark 3. After 20 minutes, turn the oven off and leave the
jars to cool slightly. Pour in your pickles while the jars are still
hot, then seal and leave to cool completely.

— PICKLED SEAFOOD —

PICKLED ANCHOVIES

SERVES 10

Maldon sea salt	25g
caster sugar	25g
fresh anchovy fillets, pinboned and scaled	40
carrot, peeled and thinly sliced	1
banana shallot, thinly sliced	1
stick of celery, thinly sliced	1
garlic clove, peeled and thinly sliced	1
Our Pickle Brine (see page 78)	250ml
interesting vinegar	
(we like white malt vinegar)	25ml

Mix together the salt and sugar in a bowl.
Layer the anchovy fillets in a plastic
container, distributing the salt and sugar
between the layers. Refrigerate for 3 hours.

Meanwhile, put the sliced vegetables into
a bowl. Bring the pickle brine to the boil
and pour over the vegetables, then leave
to cool.

Wash the anchovy fillets and arrange them
in layers in a 250ml sterilized glass
jar (see page 78), alternating with the
pickled vegetable mixture, making sure to
spread the ingredients evenly.

Put into the fridge overnight, then eat,
sprinkled with interesting vinegar.

PICKLED MACKEREL

SERVES 10

black peppercorns, crushed	5g
mustard seeds, crushed	5g
coriander seeds, crushed	5g
zest and juice of 1 orange,	
1 lemon and 1 lime	
Maldon sea salt	25g
caster sugar	25g
extremely fresh mackerel fillets, pinboned	10
carrot, peeled and thinly sliced	1
banana shallot, thinly sliced	1
stick of celery, peeled and thinly sliced	1
fresh horseradish, peeled and	
thinly sliced	2cm piece
lemon, thinly sliced	½
Our Pickle Brine (see page 78)	250ml
interesting vinegar	
(we like white malt vinegar)	25ml

Mix together the spices, citrus zests,
salt and sugar in a bowl. Layer the
mackerel fillets in a plastic container,
distributing the spice mix between the
layers. Refrigerate for 3 hours.

Meanwhile, put the vegetables and sliced
lemon into a bowl. Bring the pickle brine
and citrus juices to the boil and pour
over the vegetables, then leave to cool.

Rinse the mackerel fillets and arrange
them in layers in a 500ml sterilized glass
jar (see page 78), alternating with the
vegetable mixture, making sure to spread the
ingredients evenly.

Put into the fridge for 2 or 3 days, then
eat, sprinkled with interesting vinegar.

PICKLED SHRIMP

SERVES 10

large raw shell-on prawns	1kg
Our Pickle Brine (see page 78)	1 litre
banana shallot, thinly sliced	1
carrot, peeled and thinly sliced	1
small leek, thinly sliced	1
stick of celery, peeled and thinly sliced	1
garlic cloves, thinly sliced	2
capers, with brine	50g
mixed herbs (parsley, tarragon, thyme, bay, coriander)	small bunch
unwaxed lemon, thinly sliced	1
white peppercorns	4
pink peppercorns	4
black peppercorns	4
star anise	1
Maldon sea salt	10g
red chilli, thinly sliced	1

Peel and devein the prawns, reserving the meat until needed. Place the heads and shells in a large pan with the pickle brine and bring to a gentle simmer. Skim any impurities and continue to simmer gently for 8 minutes to make a stock.

Place all the vegetables and lemon slices in a separate pan with the reserved prawn meat, capers, herbs, spices, salt and chilli. Pass the hot prawn stock through a fine sieve into the pan, then bring back to a gentle simmer and remove from the heat immediately.

Mix well, then transfer to a 1 litre sterilized glass jar (see page 78) and leave to cool. Seal the jar, and refrigerate for a minimum of 12 hours and up to 36 hours before serving. Serve as an appetizer, with cocktail sauce or mayonnaise.

PICKLED SCALLOPS

SERVES 4

scallops, in their shells	12
Our Pickle Brine (see page 78)	1 litre
banana shallot, thinly sliced	1
carrot, peeled and thinly sliced	1
stick of celery, peeled and thinly sliced	1
garlic clove, thinly sliced	1
unwaxed lemon, thinly sliced	½
white peppercorns	4
pink peppercorns	4
black peppercorns	4
star anise	1
red chilli, thinly sliced	1
capers, with brine	10g
Maldon sea salt	5g
mixed herbs (parsley, tarragon, thyme, bay, coriander)	small bunch

Shuck the scallops, reserving the meat and scallop skirt. Put the scallop meat into a bowl and set aside. Remove the dark grit sack from the scallop skirt and discard, then rinse the skirt under cold running water until clean.

Place the scallop skirt in a pan with the pickle brine and bring up to a gentle simmer. Continue to simmer for 6 minutes to make a stock, skimming off any impurities. Put the reserved scallop meat into a separate pan with all the remaining ingredients, then pass the scallop stock through a fine sieve into the pan. Bring back to a gentle simmer, then skim any impurities again and remove from the heat.

Mix well, then transfer to a 1 litre sterilized glass jar (see page 78) and leave to cool. Seal the jar, and refrigerate for a minimum of 12 and up to 36 hours before serving.

PICKLED OYSTERS

SERVES 8

unwaxed lemon, thinly sliced	½
red chilli, thinly sliced	1
banana shallot, peeled and thinly sliced	1
black peppercorns, crushed	4
Our Pickle Brine *(see page 78)*	250ml
small rock oysters, in their shells	24
small cucumber, peeled and sliced	½

Put the lemon slices into a large heatproof bowl with the sliced chilli and shallot.

Add the peppercorns and pickle brine to a pan and bring it to the boil, then remove from the heat and pour over the lemon, chilli and shallot and allow to cool.

Shuck the oysters and rinse in cold water, reserving the meat until needed — the cold water stops the oysters forming a cloudy goo in the pickle.

When the pickle brine mix has cooled down, toss in the oysters and cucumber slices, mix well, then transfer to a 1 litre sterilized glass jar (see page 78). Seal the jar and refrigerate for a minimum of 12 and up to 48 hours. Serve with Saltine Crackers (see page 96).

— PICKLED HOT DOGS —

PICKLED SAUSAGES ARE POPULAR IN EASTERN EUROPE, BUT WE FIRST CAME ACROSS THESE IN TEXAS. EATEN COLD WITH A BEER THEY ARE HIGHLY ADDICTIVE. OUR VERSION USES HOT DOGS MADE FOR US BY OUR 'SAUSAGE GURU' STANKOV IN LONDON, BUT YOU CAN PICKLE ANY GOOD-QUALITY COOKED SAUSAGE.

MAKES 2 x 1 LITRE JARS

Our Pickle Brine *(see page 78)*	1 litre
hot dogs (such as kielbasa)	1kg
chillies	3
garlic cloves	4
sprigs of thyme	3

Put the pickle brine into a pan and bring to the boil.

Stack the hot dogs neatly in 2 large sterilized glass jars (see page 78), with the chillies, garlic and thyme spread evenly throughout the jars.

Pour over the hot pickling liquid and seal the jars. Leave to cool, then refrigerate for 1 week before eating.

BEETROOT
PICKLED EGGS

NOT JUST FOR PRESENTATION, PICKLING IN BEETROOT JUICE IMPARTS AN EARTHY FLAVOUR TO THE EGGS THAT MARRIES WELL WITH THE DEVILLED PREPARATION ON PAGE 98. THE EGGS WILL DARKEN IN COLOUR AS THEY PICKLE AND TAKE ON MORE OF THE BEET FLAVOUR THE LONGER THEY ARE IN THE JAR.

MAKES 12

small free-range Burford Brown eggs	12
Our Pickle Brine (see page 78)	700ml
beetroot juice (concentrated)	300ml

Boil the eggs for 6 minutes, then turn off the heat. Remove the eggs from the pan and roll them lightly on a work surface to give a cracked mosaic look to the shells.

Place the pickle brine and beetroot juice in a large bowl, add the eggs and allow to cool in the liquid. Refrigerate in a sterilized glass jar (see page 78) and allow to pickle for 2 days and up to 2 weeks.

To serve, remove the eggs from the liquid, peel off the shells and either eat as they are or serve in salads.

DEVILLED BEETROOT PICKLED EGGS

THE BEETROOT PICKLED EGGS ABOVE CAN ALSO BE TURNED INTO VERY SEXY DEVILLED EGGS. THE RECIPE HERE IS JUST ONE IDEA, BUT FEEL FREE TO GET CREATIVE.

Halve the beetroot pickled eggs lengthways. Scoop out the yolks and place them in a mixing bowl.

Beat the yolks with the goats' cheese, olive oil and plenty of black pepper, then pass through a fine sieve to make a smooth paste.

MAKES 12

Beetroot Pickled Eggs (see above)	6
creamy goats' cheese	50g
extra virgin olive oil	50ml
plenty of freshly ground black pepper	

Place the yolk mixture in a piping bag with a plain nozzle and pipe neatly into the egg cavities.

Refrigerate for at least 20 minutes before serving.

PICKLED SHIITAKE

WE WERE BLOWN AWAY BY THE PICKLES AT MOMOFUKU IN NEW YORK, ESPECIALLY THE SHIITAKE. THIS RECIPE IS BASED ON THOSE SAME PICKLES, WITH JUST A FEW CHANGES TO MAKE THEM STAND OUT A BIT MORE WHEN DEEP-FRIED. DRIED SHIITAKE CAN BE FOUND IN MOST ORIENTAL SUPERMARKETS. THEY CAN BE VERY SMALL AND MOSTLY STALK, SO FIND THE BIGGEST YOU CAN, OTHERWISE THE PICKLE WILL NOT BE PLEASANT. THESE PICKLED MUSHROOMS KEEP WELL AND IMPROVE WITH TIME.

MAKES 1 LITRE

dried shiitake mushrooms	200g
boiling water	2 litres
caster sugar	200g
soy sauce	275ml
cider vinegar	275ml
ginger, peeled	2cm piece
root liquorice	½ stick
star anise	½

Put the mushrooms into a container and pour over the boiling water. Place a small pan lid or plate on top of the mushrooms to keep them submerged and leave to fully rehydrate for 5–6 hours.

Remove the mushrooms from the water and discard the stalks. Cut the caps in half. Reserve 500ml of the steeping liquid and sieve it to remove any debris. Any remaining liquid can be used for stocks and sauces.

Put the mushrooms into a pan with the reserved steeping liquid and all the other ingredients. Bring to a gentle simmer, stirring occasionally and making sure the mushrooms are submerged, and cook for 30 minutes. Discard the ginger, liquorice and star anise. Leave to cool, then transfer to a sterilized jar (see page 78) and refrigerate. The pickle will be ready in 3 days, but will be better after a week.

CRISPY PICKLED SHIITAKE

SERVES 4–6

plain flour	75g
free-range eggs	3
whole milk	40ml
Japanese panko breadcrumbs	120g
Pickled Shiitake (see above), drained	400g
oil, for deep-frying	

Get ready three shallow bowls. In the first, add the flour, in the second beat the eggs with the milk, and in the third put the panko breadcrumbs. Lightly coat the pickled shiitake in flour, then dip them into the egg and milk mixture, and finally toss them carefully in the panko breadcrumbs. The shiitake should be uniformly coated. Work neatly and in small batches so that the crumbs do not become wet and clumpy. Place the mushrooms on a sheet of greaseproof paper. They freeze very well like this.

Heat the oil to 190°C in a deep-fryer and fry the shiitake for 2 minutes, until golden and crisp. Drain on kitchen paper and serve.

HOT WINGS

SERVES 4

3-joint free-range chicken wings	1kg
Master Chicken Brine *(see below)*	1 litre
House Rub *(see page 119)*	70g
unsalted butter	50g
cider vinegar	50ml
Hot Sauce or Bastard Hot Sauce	
(see pages 124 and 125)	50ml

MASTER CHICKEN BRINE

water	4 litres
Maldon sea salt	360g
interesting sugar (muscovado or maple, for instance)	120g
spice bag (dried chillies, small liquorice stick, peppercorns, star anise, cloves, cumin seeds, coriander seeds)	1
mixed herbs (thyme, bay, rosemary)	1 bunch

HOW HOT YOU MAKE THESE WINGS IS UP TO YOU. THIS RECIPE IS DEFINITELY HOT ENOUGH FOR US AND REQUIRES THE COOLING EFFECT OF A GOOD COWS' CURD AND SOME PICKLED CELERY. WE STUMBLED ACROSS A HOT SAUCE IN THE RESTAURANT THAT CAME WITH A SAFETY NOTICE AND LOOKED LIKE SATAN'S BLOOD. OUR MILK STOCKS WERE UNUSUALLY LOW THE NEXT DAY. THESE WINGS SHOULD NOT HAVE THAT EFFECT. USE THE HOT SAUCE TO TASTE. TOO HOT AND IT IS A WASTE OF GOOD CHICKEN. YOU CAN ALWAYS ADD MORE.

IF YOU ARE PARTICULAR ABOUT YOUR WINGS, REMOVE THE FIRST JOINT AND COOK IT SEPARATELY - IT MAKES FOR A MORE CIVILIZED WING AFFAIR.

To make the master chicken brine, add all the ingredients to a large pan and bring to the boil, then leave to cool. Load the wings into the brine and refrigerate for 2 hours.

Prepare a barbecue for smoking (see The Set-Up on pages 114-15) and set the temperature to 105°C.

Remove the wings from the brine and dry thoroughly on kitchen paper. Rub them all over with the house rub and shake off any excess. Smoke the wings in the barbecue for 1 hour 30 minutes, checking after 30—45 minutes and giving them a turn. They need to reach an internal temperature of at least 70°C on your meat probe. Once smoked, remove them from the barbecue.

Meanwhile, put the butter, vinegar and hot sauce into a large pan and bring to the boil. Whisk until the mixture has emulsified.

When ready to cook, adjust up the barbecue for direct grilling — you may need to add more charcoal and adjust the vents to get the temperature just hot enough to char the wings. Grill the wings until they are crispy and slightly charred, about 2 minutes each side.

Toss the wings in the hot sauce, then serve with Pickled Celery (see page 194), pickled chillies and a side of cows' curd.

· Fresh cows' curd and goats' curd work fantastically well with hot food, so don't be afraid to use them with Buffalo Pigs' Tails (see page 66) or even on top of Chipotle & Confit Garlic Slaw (see page 198). Curd is much more widely available now than a few years back, and for good reason.

KIMCHI HOT WINGS

SERVES 4

3-joint free-range chicken wings	1kg
Master Chicken Brine (see page 90)	4 litres
House Rub (see page 119)	70g
Kimchi Hot Sauce (see page 124)	200ml
oil, for deep-frying	

Load the wings into the master chicken brine and refrigerate for 2 hours.

Remove the wings from the brine and dry thoroughly with kitchen paper. Rub them all over with the house rub and shake off any excess.

Prepare a barbecue for smoking (see The Set-Up on pages 114–15) and set the temperature to 105°C. Smoke the wings in the barbecue for 1 hour 30 minutes, checking after 30–45 minutes and giving them a turn. They need to reach an internal temperature of 70°C. Once smoked, these wings can be chilled, ready for deep-frying when you are ready. If deep-frying is not your thing, a good grilling would also work well.

Put the kimchi hot sauce into a large mixing bowl. Heat the oil to 190°C in a deep-fat fryer or large saucepan and deep-fry the wings for 2 minutes, or until golden and crispy. When cooked, toss the wings in the kimchi hot sauce.

Serve with Pickled Celery (see page 194) and a side of curd. Or, if you are feeling industrious, you can pull all the meat off the wings after dressing, roll it up in lettuce leaves, dunk them in Anchovy Hollandaise (see page 174) and feel very good about yourself.

APRICOT & GREEN CHILLI WINGS

SERVES 4

3-joint free-range chicken wings	1kg
Master Chicken Brine (see page 90)	1 litre
House Rub (see page 119)	70g
oil, for deep-frying	
juice of 5 limes	
green chilli, thinly sliced	1
coriander stalks and leaves, chopped	small bunch

GLAZE

apricot jam	150g
light soy sauce	50ml
cider vinegar	25ml
Tabasco or Frank's Red Hot Sauce	25ml
green chillies, chopped into rounds	2

Load the wings into the master chicken brine and refrigerate for 2 hours.

Remove the wings from the brine and dry them thoroughly with kitchen paper. Rub them all over with the house rub and shake off any excess.

Prepare a barbecue for smoking (see The Set-Up on pages 114–15) and set the temperature to 105°C. Smoke the wings in the barbecue for 1 hour 30 minutes, checking after 45 minutes and giving them a turn. They need to reach an internal temperature of 70°C. Once smoked, remove from the barbecue, cover and chill until needed.

Combine the ingredients for the glaze in a pan over a low heat and stir until the jam has dissolved. Set aside and keep warm.

Heat the oil to 190°C in a deep-fat fryer or large saucepan and deep-fry the wings for 2 minutes, or until golden and crispy. When cooked, toss the wings in the warm glaze to coat, then drench in the lime juice. Garnish with the green chilli slices and chopped coriander and serve.

CHIPOTLE & MAPLE WINGS

SERVES 4

3-joint free-range chicken wings	1kg
Master Chicken Brine (see page 90)	1 litre

MARINADE

fennel seeds, toasted	40g
cumin seeds, toasted	10g
coriander seeds, toasted	15g
black peppercorns	40g
onion, peeled and grated	1
roasted garlic paste	50g
vegetable oil	100ml
apple juice	350ml
chipotle in adobo, puréed	75g
House Rub (see page 119)	50g
maple syrup	125g
black strap molasses	125ml
apricot preserve	150g
tomato ketchup	250ml
English mustard	100g
smoked Maldon sea salt	10g
Granny Smith apple, grated	1

Load the wings into the master chicken brine and refrigerate for 1½ hours. Meanwhile, grind the toasted seeds and peppercorns to a powder.

In a saucepan, sweat the onion and garlic paste in the oil over a high heat for 5 minutes. Add 250ml of apple juice and cook until it has reduced and evaporated. Pour the reduced mixture into a large bowl, then add all the remaining ingredients except the grated apple. Stir well to combine, then fold in the grated apple and the remaining apple juice.

Remove the wings from the brine and dry with kitchen paper. Drop the wings into the marinade and leave for 1 hour.

Prepare a barbecue for smoking (see The Set-Up on pages 114–15) and set the temperature to 105°C. Smoke the wings for 1 hour 30 minutes, checking after 45 minutes and giving them a turn. They need to reach an internal temperature of 70°C. Remove the wings and adjust the barbecue for direct grilling. Grill the wings until crisp and slightly charred, about 1–2 minutes each side, basting with any excess marinade as they cook. Serve with pickles.

BUTTER CONFIT TURKEY WINGS

SERVES 4

3-joint free-range turkey wings	1kg
Master Chicken Brine (see page 90)	1 litre
House Rub (see page 119)	70g
butter	1kg
garlic cloves, separated	2 bulbs
sprigs of thyme	5

Load the wings into the master chicken brine and refrigerate for 2 hours. Remove the wings from the brine and dry thoroughly with kitchen paper. Rub them all over with the house rub and shake off any excess.

Place in a roasting tin that fits inside your barbecue, and add the butter, garlic and thyme.

Prepare a barbecue for smoking (see The Set-Up on pages 114–15) and set the temperature to 105°C. Confit the wings by smoking them in the barbecue for 3 hours, or until they are soft to the touch. Remove the wings from the barbecue and leave to drain on kitchen paper.

When ready to cook, adjust the barbecue for direct grilling – not super-hot but just hot enough to char the wings. Grill the wings until they are crispy and slightly charred, about 2 minutes each side. Serve with Hot Sauce (see page 124) and a side of curd.

BURNT TOMATOES
— & SHALLOTS ON TOAST —

WE ARE NOT SURE IF THIS IS A
SIDE DISH, A STARTER OR JUST
A LITTLE SCOOBY SNACK FOR
WHEN HUNGER BITES — MAYBE
ALL OF THE ABOVE. IT IS ALSO
VEGETARIAN, WHICH IS A BIT OF
A SURPRISE. TOMATOES ARE THE
STAR OF THE SHOW, AND USING
GREAT TOMATOES IS THE LAW
HERE. ALSO, NEVER REFRIGERATE
TOMATOES — IT IS A SLAP IN
THE FACE OF THE TOMATO. REALLY
GOOD HOME-GROWN TOMATOES ARE
AROUND IN THE UK FOR SUCH A
SHORT TIME IN THE SUMMER, SO
TREAT THEM WELL AND YOU WILL
BE REWARDED.

SERVES 4

ripe tomatoes, at room temperature	4
banana shallots	4
lemon juice	good squeeze
extra virgin olive oil	15ml
large slices of sourdough bread, toasted	2
garlic clove, cut in half	1
Maldon sea salt	
freshly ground black pepper	

GARNISH

mint tips	1 tbsp
chive tips	1 tbsp
flat-leaf parsley, leaves picked	1 tbsp

Heat a barbecue or cast-iron griddle pan
until smoking hot.

While the grill is heating up, cut the
tomatoes in half lengthways. Peel the
shallots and halve them lengthways, keeping
the root intact. Toss the shallots in a bowl
with the tomatoes, lemon juice, olive oil,
salt and pepper, then set aside at room
temperature until the grill is hot.

Place the tomatoes and shallots, cut side
down, on the grill or griddle and leave for
a few minutes — if you move them you will
break the seal and they will leak their
juice. When slightly burnt, remove the
tomatoes and turn the shallots to colour the
other side. Keep turning the shallots for
about 6 or 7 minutes, or until cooked all
the way through.

Meanwhile, toast the sourdough, rub with the
cut sides of the garlic clove and pour over
any remaining marinade from the bowl. Place
the shallots and tomatoes on top, garnish
with the herbs and serve immediately.

SALTINE CRACKERS

IN KREUZ MARKET, JUST OUTSIDE AUSTIN, TEXAS, WE DISCOVERED THEY SERVED THEIR BARBECUE WITH SAUERKRAUT, SALSA, AVOCADOS AND THESE SALTINE CRACKERS. GENIUS. THIS IS ABOUT AS DREAMY A MOUTHFUL AS YOU WILL EVER FIND.

MAKES SHED LOADS

plain flour	250g
salt	5g
bicarbonate of soda	½ tsp
butter, chilled	25g
milk	160ml
Maldon sea salt	

Heat the oven to 200°C/400°F/gas mark 6.

Put the flour, salt and bicarbonate of soda into a bowl and grate in the chilled butter. Rub the butter into the flour using your fingertips until the mixture resembles breadcrumbs, then stir in the milk and knead lightly.

Roll out thinly, about 2—3mm thick, and place on a non-stick baking sheet. Prick with a fork, sprinkle with sea salt and cut into squares. Bake in the oven for 10 minutes, or until golden.

Serve warm topped with a slice of fresh tomato, avocado, a couple of onion rings and a slice of smoked rump or beef brisket.

DEVILLED EGGS WITH
— ROAST CHICKEN SKIN —

DEVILLED EGGS ORIGINATE FROM ROME AND WERE FIRST FOUND ALL OVER CENTRAL EUROPE IN THE NINETEENTH CENTURY. TOPPINGS WOULD VARY, DEPENDING ON THE CUISINE AND PRODUCE OF THE COUNTRY: THE RUSSIANS TOPPED A MAYONNAISE AND EGG MIXTURE WITH CAVIAR AND POTATO, THE SWEDISH USED PICKLED HERRING AND DILL, AND SO ON. WE BELIEVE THAT DEVILLED EGGS ARE GREAT IN MANY GUISES — THIS IS OUR FAVOURITE, AND MAKES FOR SOME DEVILISHLY GOOD EGGS. THIS RECIPE MAKES MORE CHICKEN SKIN THAN YOU WILL NEED — EVERYONE NEEDS EXTRA CHICKEN SKIN.

MAKES 12, ENOUGH FOR 4

large free-range hen's eggs	6
Anchovy Salad Cream *(see page 205)*	50ml
Kimchi Hot Sauce *(see page 124)*	50ml

ROAST CHICKEN SKIN

sprigs of thyme	3
chicken skins	250g
chicken stock	50ml
Maldon sea salt, to taste	

First, make the roast chicken skin. Heat the oven to 170°C/325°F/gas mark 3.

Put the sprigs of thyme into a medium-sized roasting pan and lay the chicken skins on top. Add the chicken stock, then put the pan into the oven and cook, uncovered, for 40 minutes, stirring every 10 minutes.

When the 40 minutes are up, drain off the fat and return the pan to the oven for a further 20 minutes to crisp up. The skins will not have the crunch of pork scratchings but will be like roast chicken skin. Season to taste.

Next, make the devilled eggs. Fill a pan large enough for 6 eggs with water and bring to the boil. Gently lower the eggs into the water and cook for 8 minutes. Remove the eggs, refresh under cold running water and peel off the shells.

Halve the eggs lengthways and remove the yolks to a bowl. Mix the yolks with the anchovy salad cream and pass through a fine sieve.

Arrange the halved eggs on a serving dish. Put ½ teaspoon of kimchi hot sauce into the cavity of each egg, then place the yolk mixture in a piping bag and pipe neatly into the egg cavities, on top of the sauce. Refrigerate for at least 20 minutes, then crumble the crispy chicken skin on top and serve.

HOT RIB TIPS

SERVES 2

pork rib tips (trimmed section from spare ribs)	500g
House Rub (see page 119)	70g
Barbecue Sauce (see page 122)	50ml
Hot Sauce (see page 124)	50ml
oil, for deep-frying	

Prepare a barbecue for smoking (see The Set-Up on pages 114–15) and set the temperature to 110°C.

Sprinkle the rib tips with the rub and shake off any excess.

Smoke the rib tips in the barbecue for 4–5 hours, or until they have a dark bark and are soft. Slightly overcooked is best here, as when deep-fried it is the crust that contrasts so well with the very soft meat.

Once smoked, remove the rib tips and refrigerate overnight until chilled and firm. Portion them individually (usually 3–4 from each section), then cut these in half again. The result will be about eight 5 x 2.5cm sections from each whole offcut.

Put the barbecue sauce and hot sauce into a pan and cook over a medium heat for 5 minutes, whisking to combine.

Heat the oil to 190°C in a deep-fryer or large saucepan. Add the little pieces of rib in batches and deep-fry until dark and crispy, about 2 minutes. Toss in the hot sauce and serve.

NOT EXACTLY 'TIPS', BUT THE LAST 3–4 SMALL RIBS FROM THE BACK END OF THE RIB CAGE. WE READ ABOUT PLACES IN CHICAGO SMOKING IT SEPARATELY AS LITTLE BAR SNACKS. RIBS AND BAR SNACK IN THE SAME BREATH CAN ONLY BRING HAPPINESS, RIGHT? WE TRIED THIS, BUT ALTHOUGH IT HAD SATISFYING BONE-GNAWING QUALITIES, IT WAS NOT MENU-WORTHY. AND IT REMAINED THAT WAY UNTIL ONE DAY THE LITTLE SMOKED RIBS WERE THROWN INTO THE FRYER AND TOSSED IN HOT SAUCE.

CHAPTER

03

MEATS, SAUCES {&} RUBS

MEAT SOURCING

It is for good reason that provenance – the source and origin of food – is now an integral part of good cooking and good eating. It has become fashionable to buy food from responsible sources, to know breed from breed, to know the feed and the farmer, and all this information is of huge importance when searching for the best meat to buy and cook.

We do not source meat from some of the most dedicated farmers in the country to gloat about it. It is something that drives us, fascinates us and fulfils us, and ultimately it is the meat we want to be cooking and serving to our customers. Awesome meat starts well before it gets to the butcher or the chef – it starts with the farmer, and the conscientious cook should want to know what it is they are buying and cooking. We receive the kill tag of every carcass, forequarter and rib that comes into the restaurant, with the farmer's name, kill date, age of cow and abattoir used. For us, the importance of knowing all these things cannot be underestimated. It may not interest the customers like it interests us, but they can rest easy that we know and have full confidence in the farms and farmers

that produce the food they eat. If this same approach is taken at home when sourcing your own meat, there is no doubt that over time you will have great satisfaction from eating and cooking with meat that you are proud to have purchased. This information provides not only some assurances but also fascinating information that shows just how variable meat can be.

Variances can be attributed to many things: breed; different periods of dry-ageing; the time of year that the animal was slaughtered, from when the grass is rich and lush in spring, summer and autumn to when it suffers in the lean winter months, to the cows that spend all year up on the moors or those in the wetter lowlands. Pork is also different throughout the year, with pigs laying down more fat in the winter to protect themselves from the cold. The difference is staggering, and is another point of endless fascination when carefully

sourcing your meat. We now farm our own rare-breed pigs in the village of Pitt, and it is our duty and our joy to provide them with proper husbandry and care. We are confident that our pigs could not be happier, roaming around in a huge woodland rooting and eating all the good things a big old woodland has to offer, and with a daily back-scratch and belly-rub for good measure. It is only right to buy from farms and farmers that have a similar approach to animal welfare and husbandry. Although it sounds contradictory, it is only through buying rare-breed meat from dedicated farmers that the native British rare-breed industry can grow and these passionate farmers can continue their great work.

Look for British native breeds that have been grown slowly and naturally, fed without the aid of hormones and not pumped full of grain to fuel fast growth. Good meat comes down to four main factors: genetics or breed, feed, husbandry and slaughter. The quality of the meat will be compromised when any one of these factors is neglected, and unsurprisingly the best meat will come from those farmers who value the importance of each one.

• • • • • • • • • • • • •

GENETICS

Different breeds produce different meat. Some are lean, some fat, some dark, some pale; the loins in some are long and in others they are short. Commercial pig farmers selectively cross-breed lean pigs with fast-growing pigs,

to produce large litters and large carcasses in 16–20 weeks that satisfy the supermarkets need for lean protein. Taste is secondary to profit in such circumstances. Similarly, in commercial beef farming, lean, muscle-heavy continental breeds such as Limousin and Charolais are often crossed with dairy cows and are hard-fed hormone-rich, high-protein feeds to produce a commercially viable animal for the supermarket in 15 months. The resulting beef is devoid of fat, flavour and any characteristics that may make it an enjoyable dinner prospect. This beef is simply not comparable to the slow-maturing native British breeds that are left to develop fat and muscle over 30 months and beyond. More importantly, commercial animals reared in such a way are not going to lead a happy life.

Rare-breed pigs mature and grow much more slowly than leaner commercial breeds. The natural ability to develop fat has not been bred out of them, and by the time they reach maturity they may have developed a thick layer of back fat with a prolific marbling of fat throughout the eye of the loin and into the shoulder. This is something to admire, to become giddy with excitement about and even slightly emotional over. When we picked up our first Middle White carcass from the abattoir and saw a thick, glistening layer of back fat beneath the skin, it was an amazing sight; confirmation of the inherent qualities of such pigs and justification of the sourcing of them to breed and rear. Not all rare-breed pigs are the same, however, each breed having its own particular qualities

and characteristics that become apparent when you eat the meat. There are, of course, other factors to consider than just fat development as a sign of tasty meat. Of the native British breeds, we keep Middle White and Tamworth, and have kept Berkshire in the past. All of them are beautiful pigs and have produced some of the best pork we have ever eaten. Alongside these we have focused specifically on Mangalitza, a very rare Hungarian breed introduced to the UK in 2006. While finding specific breeds of pig is an important issue when searching for the best pork, a quality rare-breed pig can only fulfil its genetic potential with the right feed, husbandry and slaughter. Only when all four things combine will you begin to eat pork as it can and really should be eaten.

Unlike pork, where we are particular in the breeds we use, we use a number of slow-maturing British breeds of beef in the restaurant and again remain perpetually fascinated by the individual characteristics and flavour profiles of each breed, raised on different types of land. Dexter, Longhorn, Shorthorn, Red Poll, Hereford, White Park, Highland, North Devon and Belted Galloway all come through the restaurant on a regular basis from a variety of farmers, and are sound bets to provide you with great beef if fed, kept and aged properly.

· · · · · · · · · · · · ·

—— FEED ——

It was an unforgettable moment when we tasted the first of the Mangalitza pigs we had reared. We had previously cooked with and eaten a lot of Mangalitza, and that was the main reason we chose to rear these beautifully furry pigs. What we produced, however, was unlike any other pork we had ever eaten – the meat was soft and dark with a thick web of marbling throughout, and had a 5cm-thick layer of hard, bright white back fat that was far sweeter, cleaner and nuttier than usual. It was the most deliciously satisfying confirmation of the importance of feed and husbandry in pig farming. The pigs had been fed cobnuts from the hazel copse in which they lived, whey from the local cheese producer, pea shoots that we sowed in the late spring and piles of old peaches and nectarines from the local vegetable market.

For us, the best beef comes from animals that have matured slowly, been allowed to eat the grass from the rich pastures on which they live and fed only with grains in the last month or so of their life to help build the decent covering of fat needed for the dry-ageing process that will shortly follow. The very best British beef is grass-fed and finished in such a way. Commercial beef, on the other hand, follows an altogether unnatural feeding process, in which the cows are fed high-protein feeds that are also high in growth hormones, antibiotics and unnatural amounts of grain, which allow the cows to develop a desirable carcass weight within a short period of time. The poor and unnatural feed compounds the poor genetics to produce very poor beef.

— OUR PIGS —

Middle White

Mangalitza

Tamworth

. . . .

— HUSBANDRY —

The unnatural feeding process of some farmers which results in animals being taken to slaughter at half the age of our animals, is an enterprise that brings fast profit and turnover, but one that produces animals of poor quality and those that can never be happy. Husbandry, the care of the animals, is a duty that the farmer must take seriously both for the welfare and happiness of the animal and the by-product of such welfare: brilliant meat.

Eat pork from free-range animals that live beyond 6 months, eat beef from cows that live beyond 25 months and eat lamb from sheep that are allowed to develop fat and flavour at 6-7 months of age.

We actually prefer hogget and mutton in the restaurant that comes from sheep that are fully mature, hogget a year old and then mutton from two years old. As with pork and beef, the flavour from older mature animals is far more developed, though the meat is slightly tougher. In all cases, try and buy from butchers who source from individual farmers. These are the people that need to be supported.

. . . .

— SLAUGHTER —

A farmer's hard work, good husbandry and passion can be undone with a poorly executed slaughter. Again, the need for a stress-free and humane slaughter is twofold. The well-being of the animal is paramount. Animals deserve to be killed in such a way that they feel no stress, but the stress that a badly run abattoir can produce in the animal also affects the quality of the meat. Stress releases hormones into the muscles of the animal, namely adrenalin, preparing it to either fight or run. If an animal is killed while it is stressed, the meat may become acidic, pale, pappy in texture and with an unnatural sheen and dark blood-red

spots throughout from blood capillaries that burst in the stressful moments before and during slaughter.

As pig keepers we could think of nothing worse than a stressful slaughter of an animal that has lived such a fulfilled life. It is simply in nobody's interest to have a stressed animal. We are very fortunate to have Laverstoke Park abattoir for our Pitt pigs, which is just a few miles up the road from us. The abattoir was designed by Temple Grundin, specifically with the animals' sensibilities in mind and consistently produces excellent carcasses for us. There are only natural curves with

no artificial light or shiny surfaces, and classical music plays throughout the process. The refrigeration is also exceptional. The carcass is not simply taken to a giant walk-in fridge after slaughter for rapid chilling, which can create something called cold shortening whereby the muscles contract to produce dry and tough meat, but is taken through a slow, gradual chilling process whereby the carcass takes 24 hours to chill fully. It is unlikely you will be able to know these things when buying from your butcher, but do look for the signs of stress in the meat and avoid it when you find them.

── DRY-AGEING ──

Ageing is vital for both maximizing flavour and texture in meat, most noticeably in beef and lamb. Pork should be hung for anything up to two weeks in order to dry the carcass, but does not benefit from long periods of ageing and is best enjoyed fresh. Beef, on the other hand, benefits immeasurably from ageing and should not be eaten fresh or if it has been wet-aged, which means it has been vacuum-bagged after butchery and left in the bag for a period of time. Wet-aged beef sits in its own blood and produces dry and unpleasant results. Dry-ageing is undoubtedly superior, but is a costly practice and is only enjoyed by a small percentage of people as a result.

After slaughter, the cow is split in two and hung in a large fridge through which air circulates quickly and freely. During the first 16–20 days of the dry-ageing process, enzymes in the meat begin to dismantle the muscle fibres, making it more tender. The meat is essentially undergoing a controlled deterioration. This tenderization then ceases, but during this subsequent period, and as the meat is hung longer, moisture loss in the meat intensifies the flavour. The slow loss of moisture, as in salami or air-dried ham production, concentrates the sweet sugars and umami-rich proteins in the meat and also allows it to retain more moisture during cooking. These concentrated molecules, and the oxidization of fat that occurs during the process, boost the 'meatiness' and umami in the meats and contribute to the spellbinding Maillard flavours (see page 108) during cooking. Meat that has been dry-aged for 25 days and beyond will have a distinctively sweet and nutty 'funk' to it, one that is entirely pleasant and very addictive. In the restaurant we put a pack of salted peanuts next to a dry-aged rib of beef and the blind

sniff test was very close. The moisture loss and the time taken for it to occur are the costly factors involved, but are also the factors that produce the flavour and texture in the meat. This is why commercial operations prefer wet-ageing – there is no moisture and weight loss in the meat, and all meat is sold by weight.

We have found that dry-aged beef also produces the best low and slow barbecue for us. Wet beef ribs tend to curl up like a double helix and dry out when smoked for long periods of time and the flavour of heavily dry-aged beef straight out of the smoker is something that cannot be replicated with inferior wet-aged beef. We like the flavour of the meat to be the dominant force in our barbecue with smoke and saucing following after, so dry-ageing has become a significant part of the restaurant. All our beef ribs are from carcasses hung for 35 days, after which the rib racks are removed and left to dry on racking for a further week or two. Our briskets are taken even further, often to 40–50 days, and we have found that this helps shorten the 'stall' (see page 116) during cooking and produces exactly the brisket we want to be eating and serving. The featherblade, which sits on the blade bone of the shoulder, we hang alongside our briskets to intensify the flavour.

When buying dry-aged beef, speak to your butcher and ask for beef that has been hung for at least 28 days. Start with 28 days and see how you like it and how it cooks. When you return, try some beef hung for 35 days and compare the two flavours. Rumps of beef can hang for up to 70 days and we enjoy our ribs of beef around 45 days depending on the breed and fat content in the animal.

· · · · · · · · · · · · ·

── PORK FAT ──

The value of pork fat cannot be underestimated; its uses are endless and the need for it in the cooking of pork is clear. When buying pork, be sure that there is both a hard thick layer of fat on top of the loin and shoulder, and a good amount of fat running through the muscle. Even if you do not intend to eat all the fat, it will aid the cooking, basting the meat as it begins to render and producing better-flavoured pork. When you bite into meat and break the muscle tissue, the fat that is embedded in the muscle, in the connective tissue, fills your mouth and this is what helps produce a juicy mouthful. This is only possible with proper fatty pork.

Fat is also a vital source of aroma and flavour in cooked meat, with the feed of the animal particularly affecting the flavour of the fat.

Our decision to start breeding Mangalitza was largely influenced by the quality of the fat and its special composition – its fat is more mono-unsaturated than any other pork fat, and higher in oleic acid than any other breed. The breed was once so highly prized for its ability to produce sweet, light and clean-tasting fat that it was traded on the Vienna stock exchange. It is interesting to note that our Mangalitza pigs benefit from 2–3 weeks hanging and it is their

special fat composition that allows this. It is an extreme lard-type pig that takes up to 20 months to mature (four times longer than most breeds), and as such produces joints of meat very high in fat that are of intense flavour and incredibly juicy. The very slow growth and high fat renders the Mangalitza about as undesirable as a pig could be for commercial pig farming and consequently was in severe danger of extinction in the 1970s. The Mangalitza is the perfect example of the value of fat in pork, and while you may not want to eat pure fat, when buying pork remember that fat will be playing the key role in the final enjoyment of a pork dish.

COLLAGEN

Different cuts of meat have varying degrees of tenderness and this can largely be attributed to the collagen in each muscle. Collagen is made of naturally occurring proteins and is the main component of connective tissue in muscle. The strength of the collagen varies in different cuts of meat and is also dependent on the age, breed and sex of the animal. Those muscles that do very little work have weak collagen. Cuts such as fillet, rib-eye, sirloin and rump all contain weak collagens and are all relatively tender.

Understanding collagen is an important part of understanding low and slow cooking. In order to turn a tough collagen-rich cut such as brisket, shin or shoulder into something delicious, juicy and tender, the muscle must be cooked with a low and even heat for a long period of time so that the collagen molecules unravel, break down and dissolve into soft gelatin that bastes and moistens the meat. This is why much barbecue requires low and slow cooking.

MAILLARD & DRIPPINGS

Maillard is the chemical reaction that occurs when meat is browned and is one of the main reasons why roasted meat tastes so delicious. While understanding the processes involved in Maillard is not necessary, understanding that it exists certainly is. Knowing that a grill needs to be hot for it to happen, and sensing when the time is right to season your steak and get it on the grill, is far more important than understanding how sugars and

amino acids in meat combine in the face of high heat to produce reactions and new flavour compounds of high awesomeness.

The reason why the flavour of grilled meat is so unique and addictive is not only down to the complex Maillard reactions that occur when meat hits a hot grill – it is, in fact, the drippings from the cooking meat and not the charcoal itself that produce the flavour

in grilled meat. When the fats, and the sugar and protein-rich juices from the meat, fall down on to the hot charcoal, they combust into smoke and flame and rise to coat the cooking meat in a multitude of unique and aromatic flavour compounds. So when you are weighing up whether to use a griddle pan or light the barbecue, know that only one will really satisfy your need for grilled meat.

{ PIG CUTS }

1	JOWL
2	BLADE
2+3	SHOULDER
3	CHUCK JOINT / SHOULDER CHOPS
4	HAND
5	HOCK
6	TROTTERS
7	BEST END
8	LOIN
9	T-BONE
10	RUMP
11	THICK END BELLY & RIBS
12	THIN END BELLY
13	LEG (HAM)

HOW IT GETS USED

LOW 'N' SLOW	GRILL
HEAD	CHUCK JOINT
JOWL	LOIN
COLLAR	RUMP
SHOULDER	SHOULDER BUTTERFLIED
HAND	SHOULDER CHOPS
HOCKS	BEST END
BELLY	LOIN CHOPS
RIBS	T-BONES
	LEG STEAKS
	HEART
	LIVER
	KIDNEYS

{ SHEEP CUTS }

1	NECK (SCRAG)
2	SHOULDER
3	SHANK
4	BEST END
5	LOIN (RACK)
6	SADDLE
7	BREAST (BELLY, RIBS)
8	LEG

HOW IT GETS USED

LOW 'N' SLOW	GRILL
NECK	BEST END
SHOULDER	SHOULDER
SHANK	RACK
HEAD	SADDLE
BREAST	RUMP
LEG	LOIN

{ COW CUTS }

1	TONGUE
2	CHEEK
3	NECK
4	BRISKET
5	SHIN
6	PLATE (SHORT RIBS)
7	FLANK
8	LEG
9	ROUND (SILVERSIDE)
10	CHUCK
11	FORERIB
12	SIRLOIN
13	T-BONE & PORTERHOUSE
14	RUMP
15	OXTAIL

HOW IT GETS USED

LOW 'N' SLOW	GRILL
CHEEKS	CHUCK (DENVER,
TONGUE	BOXEATER, FLATIRON,
NECK	UNDERBLADE FILLET)
FEATHERBLADE	RIB-EYE
BRISKET	PORTERHOUSE
RIBS	SIRLOIN
TAIL	FILLET
FLANK	RUMP CAP
PLATE (SHORT RIBS)	ONGLET
	SKIRT
SHINS	HEART
OXTAIL	

SMOKING

{ DIRECT AND INDIRECT }

WHAT DIRECT MEANS

In the UK, direct grilling is what most people think of when we say barbecue. When you have watched your old man nuking sausages, burgers and piles of helpless chicken wings, he will have been using a direct heat source, a barbecue set up for grilling. The heat from the charcoal or gas directly impacts the meat with high surface temperatures. The heat is not deflected or absorbed by anything during the cooking process and does not affect the meat solely through the convection currents in the barbecue, as it does with indirect cooking, when the barbecue is used like an oven. Direct heat should not be synonymous with burning, however, and with a little bit of skill it is one of the most exciting and important methods of cooking. Cooking over fire, whether it be direct grilling or indirect smoking, boils down to the ability to control temperature, and while it is possible to guide someone as to how this happens, it is really only something that can be learnt through time spent in the loving company of your barbecue.

When we first opened the trailer, all we had was a smoker and a grill. Both were vital cooking sources for us, used all day, every day, and represent the value in cooking directly as well as indirectly. While at the restaurant we have a charcoal grill and smokers to satisfy our need to grill and smoke simultaneously, at home this is not necessary. You can, however, put yourself in a similar position in going from cooking low and slow (indirect) to quickly finishing your meat over direct heat. We believe you get the most flavour from cooking this way, and almost all the main meat recipes following in this chapter call for finishing over a direct high heat.

The majority of barbecue books we have read (apart from those of Adam Perry Lang) skim over, or at least pay very little attention to, the importance of direct grilling over charcoal or wood. It is an essential cooking technique, and without it our menu would be half as long and our lives half as exciting. There is no way we could ever cook a pork chop in a pan on our induction stove; it just wouldn't be right. It would be boring to cook, pretty boring to eat and a bit of a turn-off.

We appreciate and enjoy the decadence of old-school French meat cookery – a côte de boeuf roasted and basted in half a litre of nutty foaming butter with garlic, shallots and thyme is a very attractive thing, and we could happily work our way through a plate of it – but it just doesn't excite in the same way that cooking directly over charcoal does and it is not the way we like to do things. While a pork shoulder smoked for 15 hours using indirect heat can be the zenith of barbecue, so can a pork chop cooked in 10 minutes. Both are barbecue and both methods deserve to be learnt and practised. Being able to cook both ways will undoubtedly make you a better person, a happier person, a sexier person and a fatter person.

We have cooked directly over charcoal every day since Pitt Cue began, and while we have all been obsessed with it for as long as we have been cooking, we still know relatively little about it and learn constantly from mistakes and from those people around us who share the passion. We are in perpetual awe of the Turkish chefs who master the raging ocakbasi, barely sweating as they feed entire restaurants from the single long grills they sit behind. We have been stopped in our tracks each time we've visited a small restaurant outside San Sebastián, where everything is cooked to perfection on handmade grills. These are people who have dedicated their lives to cooking in such a way and have become successful only through years of making mistakes and learning from them.

So, while we can give you our recipe for cooking a pork chop and advise you on how to set up a grill, all it really boils down to is practice. Just keep lighting your barbecue and cooking on it, and you will begin to understand the hot spots and cool spots on the grill; how long it takes for the coals to burn down for the optimum grilling temperature (we light the charcoal at 5pm in the restaurant for service to begin at 6pm, though arguably the best stuff comes off the grill later in the night); which brand of charcoal cooks for longest and which brand cooks at a higher temperature; and how long a full load of charcoal lasts you.

WHAT WE GRILL

There are many cuts of meat that benefit from time spent on the grill, but only a few can be covered in this book.

PIG	SHEEP	COW
shoulder joint	butterflied shoulder	chuck
butterflied shoulder	shoulder joint	Denver cut
shoulder chops	chops	boxeater
best end	rump	rib-eye
loin chops	lamb ribs	porterhouse
T bones	leg	sirloin
leg steaks	heart	fillet
rump	liver	rump
heart	kidneys	rump cap
liver		onglet
kidneys		flat iron
		underblade
		skirt
		heart

WHAT INDIRECT MEANS

Indirect cooking is how we cook low and slow. The heat source and radiant heat is never in direct reach of the meat. In the case of a ceramic barbecue, it is diffused through a thick ceramic plate. In an offset smoker, the fire pit is completely separate from where the meat is. In a kettle barbecue, a good set-up diffuses radiant heat through water trays, with the meat positioned as far away from the burning coals as possible so as to only be affected by the indirect convection currents flowing through the barbecue.

The cooking in all three types of common home barbecue works just as a convection oven does, with the heat being diffused throughout the cooking chamber so that it flows evenly around the meat while it's cooking. The cooking is therefore much more even than over direct heat. Direct heat requires constant flipping, turning and attention in order to cook evenly, while indirect heat requires a well thought-out set-up, and then beer and patience in equal measure.

WHAT WE SMOKE

Traditional barbecue would suggest that the lesser, collagen-rich cuts such as shoulder, belly, brisket, head, shins and hocks would all be best suited to indirect cooking and smoking, where the low, even heat is able to break down the collagens into gelatin without the whole cut overcooking. They all certainly favour this form of cooking and would not be pleasant if cooked quickly over a direct heat. This is how we cook these cuts, but we also like to cook many primal cuts using indirect heat for the beginning of their journey.

Cooking sections of pork loin, rump, ribs of beef and rolled shoulder to medium-rare and rare using indirect techniques before finishing them over direct heat has changed the way our menu works at the restaurant, and is perhaps the best way of using indirect heat to really benefit carefully sourced meat. So while indirect cooking has become synonymous with pulled pork, ribs and brisket, do not be limited to those.

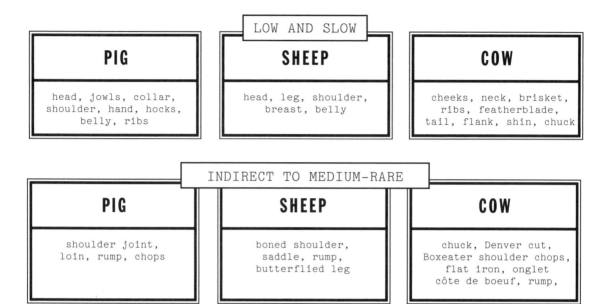

LOW AND SLOW

PIG	SHEEP	COW
head, jowls, collar, shoulder, hand, hocks, belly, ribs	head, leg, shoulder, breast, belly	cheeks, neck, brisket, ribs, featherblade, tail, flank, shin, chuck

INDIRECT TO MEDIUM-RARE

PIG	SHEEP	COW
shoulder joint, loin, rump, chops	boned shoulder, saddle, rump, butterflied leg	chuck, Denver cut, Boxeater shoulder chops, flat iron, onglet côte de boeuf, rump,

HEAT SOURCE

Barbecue at its most basic is the alchemy of wood, smoke and meat. Awesome barbecue can come from both wood and charcoal, but there is no doubt that the quality of the fuel used can dramatically affect the flavour of your final offering. It is fair to say that the best hardwood will create the best barbecue. Hardwood cells contain large amounts of lignin, which is the main reason smoked food tastes so good. When hardwood is heated, this lignin breaks down, producing new volatile chemicals that are responsible for the aromatic smoke you find in great barbecue joints, and the sweet and aromatic flavours that this smoke imparts to the meat. Hardwoods such as mesquite, oak and hickory are all high in lignin and are unsurprisingly the most common woods used in American barbecue, whereas softer woods such as pine contain low amounts of lignin and produce a bitter and acrid smoke. The huge stacks of drying hickory and white oak outside many of the best barbecue joints in Texas are testament to this fact.

At home, your best bet is to use lumpwood charcoal, made from good-quality hardwoods with none of the added chemicals that help lesser charcoals burn sufficiently well. This charcoal will become the backbone of your barbecue, the fuel that keeps the whole operation running. To this base different types and different quantities of hardwood chunks can be added, depending on the flavour profile you are looking to find.

We have used apple, mesquite, hickory and oak, and we have also dabbled with cherry wood chunks at home and in the restaurant. We like smoke to aid the flavour of the meat. The sourcing of awesome meat has always been the essence of the restaurant, and we dislike super intense and smoky barbecue where there is excessive use of mesquite or soaked wood chips. There are a load of places to find good wood chunks so try as many types of wood as possible, settling on whichever wood gives you the flavour profile you most enjoy.

THE SET-UP

There are many ways to skin a pig, and while at home we cook on both ceramic and classic kettle barbecues, it is pretty safe to say that the majority of people who want to try barbecuing will be able get their hands on a kettle barbecue, such as a Weber, a basic offset smoker or a ceramic barbecue, such as a Big Green Egg. These are what we cook on most, too, so it made

sense to gear the recipes in this book towards these types of barbecues. Nearly all these pieces of kit come with their own instructions, but the following methods are what have worked best for us and are widely used by the most avid home cooks.

Good barbecuing is all about being able to control the heat on the barbecue you are using, understanding what is happening at different temperatures and the benefits of cooking at those temperatures. This comes naturally the more you cook, but setting up a two-zone barbecue will stand you in good stead. The set-up is very simple, and basically means that one side of your grill is hot, producing direct heat that allows for fast grilling and for the important Maillard reactions to happen, while the other side of the grill produces none of its own heat but relies on the convection heat currents in the barbecue to create indirect heat and the kind of temperatures that are ideal for smoking.

By controlling the temperature of your barbecue using the air vents, you will be able to begin implementing the techniques that we use in the restaurant for both the primal cuts that are taken to medium-rare and the lesser cuts that come out of the smoker low and slow. This set-up also provides a safety net if you have a super-fatty piece of meat and do not want to suffer the mega flare-ups that could ruin something so special. Being able to moderate the cooking using two different zones is particularly helpful if this is the case. Our robata grill in the restaurant works in a similar way. If the grill is getting a bit angry and beautiful things are at risk of burning, we just sit them on the top level of the grill, right at the back, where they can rest and take stock until the grill begins to behave again.

The aim with your two-zone set-up is to have two very different temperatures at either side of your grill. Ideally, the indirect zone will hover at around 105–130°C and the direct zone will sit at around 170–190°C. Keeping the temperature at 107–110°C, the magical temperatures for much great low and slow cooking, is most definitely not essential, but keeping the temperature as constant as possible within these basic guidelines will definitely help and allow you to begin to get an idea of how long different cuts are going to take to cook when you come to trying them again. We have tasted some unbelievable meat at various barbecue competitions where smokers were being set to 130°C and upwards, but these people were militant in their checking and had honed their recipes over many years. Stick to 105–125°C and you cannot go too far wrong.

To achieve this you need to fill up a chimney starter with charcoal, light the charcoal and wait until ready to use (white, ash-covered coals in the best sign) before pushing all the lit coals to one side of the bottom ash grate in the barbecue. Place an aluminium tray filled with hot water next to the coals on the other side of the barbecue, then put the grill grate on and place another aluminium water-filled tray on the grill grate directly above the coals. You can now cook indirectly on the other side of the grill grate, next to the top water tray. The two water trays will help moderate the heat from the coals and also provide an important source of moisture when cooking. The right humidity in the barbecue is very important. Cooking large volumes in one smoker creates a very humid cooking atmosphere, and often produces a moister and faster-cooked product. The water trays are there to help this when cooking only one or two things for a long period of time at home. You are now ready to cook indirectly. Add a few wood chunks over the lit coals in order to begin smoking.

CONTROL

Keeping the temperature constant is the biggest challenge when smoking at home. The vents at the bottom of the barbecue are the key and should be used to effect oxygen intake, which in turn dictates how fast and how hot the coals burn. Opening the bottom vents in the barbecue will increase the air flow, or draught, sucking more oxygen-rich air into the fire and causing it to burn fiercer and faster. Closing the bottom vents will reduce the draught and the oxygen that reaches the fire, causing it to cool and burn more slowly. The ability to control the temperature through the manipulation of draught and oxygen is the goal.

In the search for complete temperature control, the top vents are less significant and do not provide the same control as the bottom vents. The top vents do affect the draught, however, and how easy it is for the smoke and air to leave the barbecue. The top vents should remain half open to allow for draught, and to avoid excessive build-up of smoke in the barbecue, which creates acrid, sooty deposits and could ruin your hard work. Start with the bottom vents fully open, to allow the coals to get going. You will see the temperature begin to rise, and as you begin to reach 100°C, close the vents by half. This should halt the rise in temperature, and from here it is a case of tweaking to get to your desired temperature for low and slow. The top vents need not be played with too much, but positioning the meat directly above the vents will force the smoke over the meat, and also allow you to poke a thermometer through the vents to where the meat is cooking so that you can work out exactly what temperature the most important part of the barbecue is at.

For larger cuts, like brisket, shoulder and most definitely suckling pig, you will have to be prepared to light the chimney starter on numerous occasions to maintain the lit charcoal in the barbecue. The general rule of thumb is to add six chunks of lit coal every hour. This should help maintain a constant temperature. Adding unlit coals is fine – it just prolongs any dip in temperature. This is where a ceramic barbecue becomes very useful, with one load of charcoal lasting longer than you will ever really need to cook a single large joint.

S M O K I N G

G R I L L I N G

WHEN IS IT READY?

This is one of the most important questions. While cooking something for half a day at a low temperature provides the cook with greater margin for error, removing the meat from your barbecue at the right time is crucial. There are so many variables in cooking outdoors: the insulation of your barbecue, the weather, the fuel and the genetics of the animal all play a key role in how a piece of meat is going to cook. Timings for our recipes are approximate in the loosest sense, and need to be taken with a fistful of salt. This may sound stupid for a cookbook, and maybe it is, but barbecue is far from an exact science and that's just the way it is. As long as you have a meat probe to hand, use the timings as a guide and use 'the force', you will be just dandy.

Probes are invaluable tools, but touch should not be forgotten, especially when cooking over direct heat. This is something that becomes apparent purely through experience, although using touch and a probe alongside each other will allow you to train your touch without too many cock-ups. There is no shame at all in using a meat probe, and it is really the only way to produce consistent barbecue straight away. If possible, buy a remote meat probe that allows you to read the internal temperature without lifting the lid of the barbecue. Lifting the lid releases all the moisture from the cooking chamber and

drops the temperature. Our friend David calls this 'peeking', and is convinced that it is the root of all evil. The more moisture that is retained inside your barbecue, the better, so a remote probe is a great tool to have.

One time where 'peeking' usually becomes rife is when the meat 'stalls' or 'plateaus'. When the meat reaches an internal temperature of roughly 70°C, it stops and may not rise a degree in temperature for an hour or so. This is when people sweat a little and start to panic. The barbecue is then opened, the meat is checked and the vents are opened to try to force the temperature up. These are all bad moves. The stall in temperature is standard and occurs when the collagen begins to break down into gelatin. The reaction absorbs energy and forces moisture to the surface of the meat, which cools it. These panic reactions lose more moisture and temperature in the cooking chamber and only contribute to a longer stall. Some people 'crutch' when this occurs, which means wrapping the meat in foil, often with some fruit juice, butter and stock, and returning it to the smoker to speed through the stall. Some people believe this creates a moister end result, which is no surprise as it is essentially a braise, but it prevents a decent bark from forming. It is up to you. We do not bother with it.

```
┌─────────────────────────────────────────────┐
│        DIRECT INTERNAL TEMPERATURES           │
│              45° C – BLEU                      │
│              50° C – RARE                      │
│           55° C – MEDIUM-RARE                  │
│             60° C – MEDIUM                     │
│       170° C – WHERE MAILLARD BEGINS           │
│                                               │
│           INDIRECT TEMPERATURES               │
│             70° C – THE STALL                  │
│  85–90° C – TIME TO REMOVE THE MEAT FROM THE SMOKER │
│      110° C – IDEAL COOKING TEMPERATURE        │
└─────────────────────────────────────────────┘
```

PITT CUE MISE-EN-PLACE

There really is no set armoury for barbecue – in its purest form, fire and something with which to support the meat over the fire is all that is really needed. But we have evolved from caveman dining (sort of), and the modern-day cook seeks comfort and assurance when setting out to make dinner, so there are a few things that will help you get started and ensure that cock-ups are few and far between. A lot of barbecue is winging it, and this seems to have worked for us so far, but beyond experience there are a few key tools to push you forward:

ESSENTIALS

A SOLID BARBECUE — A decent barbecue is a pretty essential starting point. Whether you go ceramic (Big Green Egg), kettle (Weber), gas, offset or fancy building yourself a pit, just make sure you are not setting yourself up for a fall before you even begin — you do not have to remortgage your house to cook solid barbecue.

CHARCOAL — Natural hardwood lump charcoal.

HARDWOOD — Not a euphemism. Source chunks of good hardwood (e.g. oak, hickory).

HEAVY CAST-IRON GRILL GRATE — For direct grilling, a good surface is essential, as it retains heat better and aids in the all-important quest for Maillard.

CHIMNEY STARTER — If you are cooking on a Weber-style barbecue, this is essential. Unsurprisingly, Weber themselves make the best one. Clever chaps.

INSTANT-READ MEAT PROBE — Meat probes will save you a huge amount of headache in the long run. We smoke a lot of bigger cuts to medium-rare or rare in the restaurant smokers, and having a meat probe can be a real life-saver. The following recipes are all written with a meat probe in mind, so unless 'the force' is super strong you may struggle.

ALUMINIUM WATER TRAYS — Source the 30 x 15cm containers.

YOUR MITTS — The more you cook, the more important touch becomes. With time you will be able to know through touch when a steak is rare and when a brisket is reaching perfection. Never underestimate your mitts.

SQUEEZY BOTTLES

TONGS

TORCHON

APRON

AWESOME KNIFE

RUBS

THESE RUBS ARE ESSENTIAL TO BARBECUE AND ARE BASED ON WHAT MEAT YOU PLAN TO SMOKE, BUT THEY CAN AND SHOULD BE ADJUSTED TO SUIT YOUR TASTE AND INTRIGUE.

BEEF RUB

MAKES 350G

Maldon sea salt	200g
maple sugar or soft light brown sugar	70g
English mustard powder	25g
hot smoked paprika	25g
freshly ground black pepper	25g

Blitz all the ingredients in a blender. Store in an airtight container for up to 1 week.

PORK RUB

MAKES 350G

Maldon sea salt	200g
maple sugar or soft light brown sugar	140g
fennel seeds, toasted	25g
freshly ground black pepper	25g
sage leaves	10g
rosemary leaves	10g
garlic cloves	25g

Blitz all the ingredients in a blender and spread on a clean tray to dry. Blitz again, then store in an airtight container. Keeps for up to 1 week.

LAMB RUB

MAKES 350G

Maldon sea salt	200g
maple sugar or soft light brown sugar	75g
English mustard powder	25g
fennel seeds, toasted	25g
garlic cloves	25g
rosemary leaves	10g
thyme leaves	10g
zest of 1 lemon	

Blitz all the ingredients in a blender. Store in an airtight container for up to 1 week.

DUCK RUB

MAKES 325G

Maldon sea salt	200g
maple sugar or soft light brown sugar	75g
black peppercorns	25g
fennel seeds, toasted	10g
star anise	10g
stick of cinnamon	10g
zest of 1 orange	

Blitz all the ingredients in a blender. Store in an airtight container for up to 1 week.

HOUSE RUB

MAKES 300G

fennel seeds	10g
cumin seeds	1 tsp
black peppercorns	1 tsp
coriander seeds	1 tsp
soft dark brown sugar	100g
granulated sugar	50g
garlic powder	10g
fine salt	100g
smoked paprika	15g
paprika	30g
dried oregano	1 tsp
cayenne	1 tsp

Toast the fennel seeds, cumin seeds, peppercorns and coriander seeds in a dry pan over a medium heat for a few minutes, shaking the pan, until the spices release an aroma. Tip into a bowl and leave to cool.

Blitz the toasted spices in a blender to a rough powder. Combine with the remaining ingredients and mix thoroughly. Keep in a sealed container for up to 1 week.

PENNY BUN RUB

MAKES 300G

dried ceps (or shiitake if not available)	100g
Maldon sea salt	100g
light muscovado sugar	100g
smoked paprika	1 tsp
freshly ground black pepper	1 tsp

Blitz the dried mushrooms to a powder (a coffee grinder will work best). Mix with all the other ingredients and store in an airtight container. Rub it on beef or use as a seasoning.

SMOKED BACON RUB

MAKES 400G

smoked bacon	200g
smoked Maldon sea salt	100g
maple sugar or soft light brown sugar	100g
freshly ground black pepper	pinch
hot smoked paprika	pinch
freshly ground anise seed	pinch

Heat the oven to 180°C/350°F/gas mark 4. Get ready two heavy metal trays and two sheets of greaseproof paper.

Sandwich the bacon between the greaseproof sheets and the two trays and bake in the oven for 30 minutes, or until brown and crispy. Remove from the oven and lay the bacon on kitchen paper to cool and dry out.

Use a pestle and mortar to grind the dry bacon to a fine powder with the remaining ingredients. Spread out on a clean tray to dry further. When completely dry, grind once more and put into airtight jars. Once a jar has been opened, use within 1 week.

DRY CURE

MAKES 1.25KG

salt (a 50:50 mix of Maldon sea salt and smoked Maldon sea salt is a winner)	1kg
molasses sugar	150g
cracked black pepper	10g
star anise, finely ground	1
fennel seeds, toasted and crushed	10g

Mix all the ingredients in a bowl until they are thoroughly combined.

SAUCES

MOTHER SAUCE

MAKES 2.5 LITRES

dry-aged beef trim, diced	500g
beef stock	1 litre
pork stock	1 litre
shallots, finely diced	5
butter	50g
sweet Madeira	200ml
tomato ketchup	200ml
French's mustard	60ml
cider vinegar	25ml
Worcestershire sauce	40ml
Tabasco	1 tsp
cloudy apple juice	100ml
blackstrap molasses	50ml
pork dripping (meat jelly from the smoking)	100g

WE HAVE A MOTHER SAUCE AT THE RESTAURANT. THE AIM OF THIS WAS TO PRODUCE THE MEATIEST OF ALL SAUCES. NOT SWEET OR ACIDIC, LIKE A BARBECUE SAUCE, BUT A SAUCE SO PACKED WITH UMAMI AND SMOKY MEATINESS THAT YOU WOULD TASTE IT HOURS LATER.

Brown the dry-aged beef trim in a large pan over a high heat until well browned. Add both stocks and deglaze the pan, then lower the heat and simmer, skimming the surface continuously, until the liquid has reduced by two-thirds.

Meanwhile, in another pan, sweat the shallots in the butter for about 5-8 minutes, or until soft. Add the Madeira, bring to a simmer and reduce the liquid by half.

Add the Madeira mixture to the reduced stock and simmer to reduce the liquid by a further quarter, skimming continuously.

Mix together all the remaining ingredients, except the pork dripping, and add to the pan. Finally, whisk in the pork dripping until combined.

Pass the mixture through a fine sieve before using to baste meat before serving.

BARBECUE JELLY

MAKES APPROXIMATELY 400G

black peppercorns	2 tsp
fennel seeds	2 tsp
mustard seeds	2 tsp
red peppers, deseeded	2
chipotle chillies, split	2
ripe tomatoes	2
cooking apples, peeled and cored	2
maple syrup	100ml
cider vinegar	100ml
smoked Maldon sea salt	2 tsp
pectin	1 sachet (8g)

Toast the peppercorns, fennel seeds and mustard seeds in a dry frying pan over a medium heat for a few minutes, shaking the pan, until the spices release an aroma. Remove from the heat and crush with a mortar and pestle.

Chop the peppers, chillies, tomatoes and apples roughly and place in a stainless steel preserving pan with the maple syrup, vinegar and salt.

Bring to the boil, then reduce the heat and simmer for 1 hour. Pour into a jelly bag and hang over a bowl overnight.

Put the resulting clear juice with the pectin into the preserving pan and boil, skimming as you go, until the mixture reaches a setting point of 105°C on a sugar thermometer.

Decant into a 500ml sterilized jar (see page 78) and cover the exposed surface at the top of the jar with a circle of waxed paper. This makes a great accompaniment for all types of cooked meat.

PITT CUE BARBECUE SAUCE

THANKS TO BIG CONGLOMERATE BURGER JOINTS, BARBECUE SAUCE IS PERHAPS MORE WELL KNOWN AND RECOGNIZED THAN THE CUISINE, AND THE TECHNIQUES OF THAT CUISINE, FROM WHICH IT COMES. THIS IS NOT A FAIR REPRESENTATION OF BARBECUE SAUCE OR THE MANY VARIATIONS IN WHICH IT IS FOUND IN EACH OF THE BARBECUE REGIONS OF AMERICA. CLASSIFYING BARBECUE INTO DISTINCT REGIONS IS PROBLEMATIC. YOU CAN SAFELY SAY, HOWEVER, THAT THE SAUCES IN THE CAROLINAS WILL VARY FROM THOSE IN MEMPHIS, KANSAS AND TEXAS, BUT WHAT IS PERHAPS MOST NOTICEABLE FROM TRAVELLING AROUND THE SOUTHERN STATES IS THAT EVERYONE MAKES THEIR OWN SAUCE, STAMPING IT WITH THEIR OWN IDENTITY AND PERSONALITY. THIS IS PART OF THE INTRIGUE OF VISITING DIFFERENT PLACES. THE BASE OF THE SAUCE MAY BE SIMILAR ACROSS ONE REGION BUT THE FINAL PRODUCTS IN EACH BARBECUE JOINT ARE WORLDS APART. THIS IS OUR SAUCE, BASED ON NO REGION IN PARTICULAR.

MAKES 1 LITRE

vegetable oil	25ml
white onion, peeled and grated	1
garlic clove, peeled and grated	1
Spice Mix *(see below)*	25g
apple juice	125ml
cider vinegar	125ml
maple syrup	135ml
French's mustard	125ml
blackstrap molasses	125ml
apricot preserve	125ml
Chipotle Ketchup *(see page 125)*	500ml
smoked Maldon sea salt	25g

SPICE MIX

fennel seeds	5g
cumin seeds	5g
coriander seeds	5g
celery seeds	5g
mustard seeds	5g
black peppercorns	5g

To make the spice mix, toast all the spices in a dry pan over a medium heat for a few minutes, shaking the pan until golden. Tip into a bowl and leave to cool. Blitz the toasted spices in a blender to a rough powder.

Heat the vegetable oil in a pan over a medium heat. Add the onion, garlic and spice mix and cook gently for 10 minutes, or until the onions are cooked through. This is important, as undercooked onions will taint the final sauce with an unpleasant raw onion flavour. Add the apple juice and cider vinegar and simmer until reduced by a third.

Add the remaining ingredients, bring to a simmer and continue to simmer for 5 minutes.

Blitz the sauce with an immersion blender, then pass it through a fine sieve. Pour into a 1 litre sterilized bottle (see page 78). Once cool, store in the refrigerator and use within 2 weeks.

HOT SAUCE

MAKES APPROXIMATELY 500ML

red peppers	1kg
red chillies	250g
Maldon sea salt	5g
cider vinegar	25ml
maple syrup	25ml
garlic cloves	25g

Prepare a barbecue for smoking (see The Set-Up on pages 114—15) and set the temperature to 120°C.

Smoke the peppers in the barbecue for 2 hours, or until soft. Discard the skins and as many seeds as possible, then put the flesh into a saucepan.

Adjust the barbecue for direct grilling or heat a griddle pan on the hob until smoking hot, and grill the chillies until blackened. Remove the stalks, then add the whole chillies, skins and all, to the peppers. Add the rest of the ingredients to the pan, bring to a simmer and cook over a low heat for 30 minutes.

Put the mixture into a blender and blitz until well mixed but still a little chunky. Decant into a 500ml sterilized jar or bottle (see page 78) and refrigerate. The sauce will keep for 1 week in the fridge.

KIMCHI HOT SAUCE

MAKES 1 LITRE

caster sugar	100g
garlic cloves, peeled	100g
spring onions, white parts only	100g
carrots, peeled and roughly chopped	100g
fresh ginger, peeled and roughly chopped	100g
Korean chilli powder	100g
anchovy fillets	100g
light soy sauce	100ml
Tay Ninh salt chilli shrimp	100g
water	200ml

Put all the ingredients into a blender and process to a smooth purée. Pass through a fine sieve and pour into a 1 litre sterilized bottle (see page 78).

This sauce will naturally ferment over time, so keep it in the fridge and use within 2 weeks. This sauce also acts as a base for other things: kimchi hollandaise is particularly awesome.

BASTARD HOT SAUCE

MAKES APPROXIMATELY 500ML

red peppers	1kg
Scotch bonnet chillies	250g
Maldon sea salt	5g
cider vinegar	25ml
maple syrup	25ml
garlic cloves	25g

Prepare a barbecue for smoking (see The Set-Up on pages 114–15) and set the temperature to 120°C.

Smoke the peppers in the barbecue for 3–4 hours, or until soft. Remove the skins and as many seeds as possible and put the flesh into a bowl.

Adjust the barbecue for direct grilling or heat a griddle pan on the hob until smoking hot, and grill the Scotch bonnet chillies until blackened. Remove the green stalks, then add the whole chillies, skins and all, to the peppers. Add the rest of the ingredients.

Put the mixture into a blender and blitz until well mixed but still a little chunky. Decant into a 500ml sterilized jar or bottle and refrigerate. The sauce will keep for 1 week in the fridge.

CHIPOTLE KETCHUP

MAKES APPROXIMATELY 1 LITRE

ripe tomatoes, chopped	1kg
onions, peeled and chopped	250g
cooking apples, peeled, cored and chopped	250g
chipotle peppers	250g
cider vinegar	250ml
smoked Maldon sea salt	25g
hot smoked paprika	25g
light muscovado sugar	250g

Place all the ingredients except the muscovado sugar in a stainless steel pan and bring to a gentle simmer. Continue to cook at a simmer for 2 hours, then pass through a vegetable mouli.

Return the mixture to the pan with the muscovado sugar and continue cooking for around 30 minutes, or until thickened, stirring regularly to prevent catching.

Decant into sterilized bottles or jars (see page 78) and seal. When cool, refrigerate for a few days before using. Use within 2 weeks.

— FRUIT KETCHUPS —

APPLE KETCHUP

MAKES APPROXIMATELY 400ML

Granny Smith apples, peeled, cored and very thinly sliced	350g
caster sugar	150g
cider vinegar	150ml
vanilla pod	½
lemon juice	10ml

Put the apples, sugar, vinegar and vanilla pod into a stainless steel pan and bring to the boil. Continue to cook for roughly 10 minutes, or until the apples are very soft.

Drain the apples, reserving the liquid, and remove the vanilla pod. Put the fruit into a blender and blitz to a thick purée, adding the lemon juice and enough of the reserved hot pickling liquid to get the correct apple sauce consistency. It should be a smooth purée that holds its shape when on a plate.

Pass the sauce through a sieve and refrigerate until needed.

WHITE PEACH KETCHUP

MAKES APPROXIMATELY 400ML

white peaches, peeled, stoned and very thinly sliced	350g
caster sugar	75g
cider vinegar	150ml
lemon juice	10ml

Put the peaches, sugar and vinegar into a stainless steel pan and bring to the boil, then continue to cook for roughly 10 minutes, or until the peaches are very soft.

Drain the peaches, reserving the liquid. Put the fruit into a blender and blitz to a thick purée, adding the lemon juice and enough of the reserved hot pickling liquid to get the correct consistency. It should be a smooth purée that holds its shape when on a plate.

Pass the sauce through a sieve and refrigerate until needed.

PEAR & MEAD KETCHUP

MAKES APPROXIMATELY 400ML

pears, peeled, cored and very thinly sliced	350g
caster sugar	130g
cider vinegar	150g
lemon juice	10ml
mead	20ml

Put the pears, sugar and vinegar into a stainless steel pan and bring to the boil, then continue to cook for roughly 10 minutes, or until the pears are very soft.

Drain the pears and reserve the liquid. Put the fruit into a blender and blitz to a thick purée, adding the lemon juice, the mead and enough of the reserved hot pickling liquid to get the correct consistency. It should be a smooth purée that holds its shape when on a plate.

Pass the sauce through a sieve and refrigerate until needed.

PINEAPPLE & CHILLI KETCHUP

MAKES APPROXIMATELY 400ML

pineapple flesh, very thinly sliced	300g
caster sugar	100g
cider vinegar	150ml
lemon juice	10ml
red chilli, very finely diced	½

Put the pineapple, sugar and vinegar into a stainless steel pan and bring to the boil, then continue to cook for roughly 10 minutes, or until the pineapple is very soft.

Drain the pineapple, reserving the liquid. Put the fruit into a blender and blitz to a thick purée, adding the lemon juice and enough of the reserved hot pickling liquid to get the correct consistency, then fold in the diced chilli. It should be a smooth purée with flecks of chilli that holds its shape when on a plate.

Pass the sauce through a sieve and refrigerate until needed.

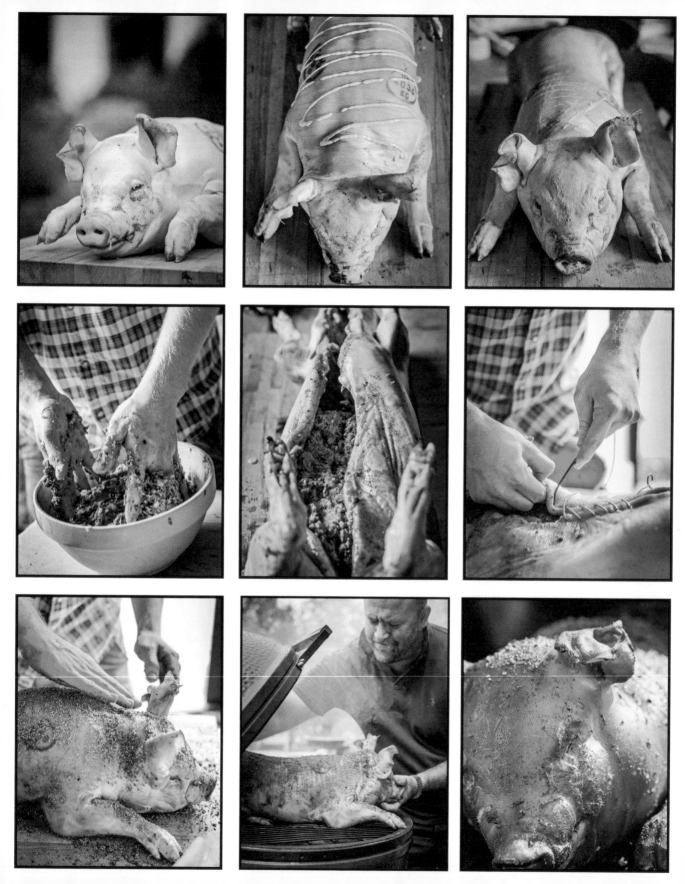

PIG DIP
—— (WHOLE LOW 'N' SLOW SMOKED SUCKLING PIG) ——

SERVES 15 HUNGRY INDIVIDUALS

pork dripping	100ml
onions, peeled and sliced	4
garlic cloves, crushed	2
kidneys from the suckling pig, chopped	2
loaf of bread, cut into 2cm cubes	½
apple, grated	1
Devil Dip Gravy *(see page 130)*	
Porger Sausage meat, uncooked	
(see page 155)	1kg
whole suckling pig, gutted, cleaned,	
singed and shaved 1, weighing about	10kg
smooth mustard of choice	100g
House Rub *(see page 119)*	200g

TO SERVE

Potato Rolls *(see page 240)*
Kimchi *(see page 214)*
slaw of choice *(see pages 198–203)*
Pitt Cue Barbecue Sauce *(see page 122)*
Baked Beans *(see page 239)*
Bibb Lettuce & Herb Salad *(see page 209)*

FOR US, A BARBECUE SUCKLING PIG IS RIGHT UP THERE ON THE AWESOME SCALE. BIG FEASTING DISHES ARE A GREAT WAY TO ENJOY AN EVENING, AND THEY GIVE YOU THE GUILT-FREE OBLIGATION OF PUTTING TOGETHER AS MANY SIDE DISHES, SAUCES AND PICKLES AS HUMANLY POSSIBLE TO SIT ALONGSIDE THE FINE BEAST IN THE CENTRE OF THE TABLE. SUCKLING PIGS ARE EASILY AVAILABLE FROM GOOD BUTCHERS, WILL JUST ABOUT FIT INSIDE YOUR BARBECUE AND ARE INCREDIBLY EASY TO COOK. SMOKING THE SUCKLING PIG WILL NOT GIVE TEXTBOOK CRACKLING, BUT IT HAS VERY ENJOYABLE SMOKY CHEWING QUALITIES OF ITS OWN.

Melt the pork dripping in a large pan and cook the onions and garlic over a medium heat until soft. Add the chopped kidneys, the cubed bread and the grated apple, and a ladle of devil dip gravy to moisten the mix, then set aside to cool.

Put the sausage meat into a bowl and add the cooled kidney mixture. Stuff into the cavity of the pig and sew the belly together using a large needle and butcher's thread.

Score the skin of the pig and rub with mustard, then rub from head to toe with the house rub.

Prepare a barbecue for smoking (see The Set-Up on pages 114–15) and set the temperature to 150°C.

Place the pig in the barbecue belly down and with the legs tucked underneath. A 10kg pig will take around 8–10 hours to smoke, and should reach an internal temperature at the shoulder of around 86°C when cooked. Some of the skin around the rump of the pig may begin to tear and pull away. If you gently poke the exposed flesh, you will gain a good idea of whether the pig is cooked through — it should be soft to the touch, similar to a pulled pork shoulder.

Transfer the pig to a large wooden board and leave to rest for 30–45 minutes. Then pull it apart and make sandwiches of the pork with the potato rolls kimchi, slaw and barbecue sauce, dipping them into the devil dip gravy as you eat. Serve alongside the baked beans and a fresh Bibb lettuce salad. Depending on the efficiency of your dipping technique, this feast may require several metres of napkin.

DEVIL DIP GRAVY

THIS IS THE MOTHER OF ALL GRAVIES, THE GRAVY TO WHICH ALL OTHER GRAVIES MUST BOW DOWN. IT PROVIDES A GREAT DIP FOR ALMOST ANY BUN OR HOT DOG. JUST BE SURE YOU MAKE A LOT.

SERVES 8–10

chicken wings, chopped	200g
chicken skin, chopped	200g
vegetable oil	10ml
shallots, chopped	4
garlic clove	1
button mushrooms, chopped	100g
sprig of thyme	1
small bay leaf	1
mixed peppercorns, crushed	10g
chipotle paste or Chipotle Ketchup	
(see page 125)	10g
Madeira	100ml
white wine vinegar	100ml
chicken gravy	500ml
beef gravy	500ml

TO FINISH

mustard	100g
butter	100g

Heat the oven to 170°C/325°F/gas mark 3. Put the chopped chicken wings and chicken skin on a baking tray and roast for 30 minutes, or until golden.

Heat the oil in a large pan and sauté the shallots and garlic. Add the roast chicken wings and skin, the mushrooms, thyme, bay leaf, crushed peppercorns and chipotle paste, and continue to cook until caramelized.

Add the Madeira and vinegar, then simmer to reduce by half before adding the chicken and beef gravies. Simmer for 30 minutes, then pass through a fine sieve and set aside.

Blend the mustard with the butter. When ready to serve, reheat the gravy and whisk in the mustard butter to taste.

PULLED PIG'S
—— HEAD CRUBEENS ——

PULLED PIG'S HEAD IS VERY SIMILAR TO PULLED PORK, JUST A TOUCH MORE
FATTY, DEPENDING ON HOW BIG YOUR PIG'S JOWLS ARE. THE CRUBEEN WAS A CLEAR
PROGRESSION FROM THE PULLED PIG'S HEAD AND FULFILLED OUR NUGGET LOVE.
THIS IS BEST SERVED WITH KIMCHI IN A BUN — KIMCHI IS A GREAT COMPANION
TO THE FATTY SMOKINESS OF THE CRUBEEN.

SERVES 4

fresh pig's head, shaved, singed, split and well rinsed	1
Pork Rub (see page 118), plus extra to season	100g
Devilled Pigs' Feet (see page 145)	200g
parsley leaves, finely chopped	handful
oil, for deep-frying	
plain flour, sifted	100g
large free-range eggs	2
whole milk	40ml
Japanese panko breadcrumbs	200g
salt and pepper	

Prepare a barbecue for smoking (see The Set-Up on pages 114–15) and set the temperature to 105–110°C.

Take your pig's head and, depending on the size of the head, remove the skin from the jowls and score the cheeks. Remove the ears and reserve them for making crispy Habanero Pigs' Ears (see page 64). Apply the pork rub all over, shaking off any excess, and then place it in your barbecue to smoke. The head can take anywhere between 10–12 hours to smoke, but it is very forgiving. It is better to wait longer than to rush and remove the head early. The meat needs to be meltingly soft for the crubeens, so please be patient. Alternatively, roast in the oven at 140°C/275°F/gas mark 1 for 6–8 hours.

Remove the head when the deepest part of the cheek reaches an internal temperature of 90°C.

Allow the cheek to cool slightly so that it can be pulled apart. Discard the tough, hard skin and remove all the meat from behind the eyes and cheekbones, along with the jowl and any scraps of meat and fat you can find, putting it all into a bowl. Mix the devilled pigs' feet through the head meat, add the parsley and season with the remaining pork rub to taste.

Spread three layers of clingfilm on a work surface and place the meat mixture on top. Mould it into a long sausage, then roll the clingfilm over it. Roll tightly from each end of the clingfilm until firm. Chill in a container of water in the refrigerator for several hours. Cut into 1cm discs, then remove the clingfilm. Alternatively, for a pig's head bun, as in the photograph opposite, roll into a sausage the width of your buns, chill as above and slice into 2cm discs.

Get ready three shallow bowls. In the first put the flour, in the second beat the egg with the milk, and in the third put the panko crumbs. Roll the discs first in flour, then coat with the egg mixture, then lightly coat in the panko crumbs — the discs should be evenly coated. Heat the oil to 190°C in a deep-fryer or a large saucepan. Carefully drop them into the oil in batches and deep-fry for 2–3 minutes, or until golden. Drain on kitchen paper, then serve, either on their own as a snack or in Potato Rolls or London Bath Buns (see page 240) with Kimchi (see page 214) and Hot Sauce (see page 124).

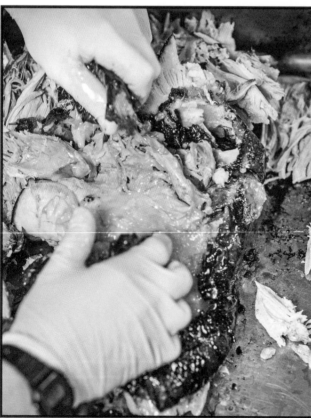

— PULLED PORK SHOULDER —

MAKES ENOUGH FOR 16 SANDWICHES

pork neck end shoulder	1, weighing 4-5kg
House Rub *(see page 119)*	250g
Mother Sauce *(see page 120)*	200ml
Maldon sea salt	
freshly ground black pepper	

> PULLED PORK WAS HOW PITT CUE STARTED. OUR SMOKER WAS SMALL AND OUR MENU REFLECTED IT. OFFERING JUST PULLED PORK A LOT OF THE TIME MEANT IT HAD TO BE GOOD. USING WOODLAND-REARED, FREE-RANGE PIGS WAS A GOOD START, BUT KEEPING IT SIMPLE WAS THE KEY. THE PULLED PORK MUST BE SOFT AND MELTING, WITH NUGGETS OF SWEET BARK DOTTED THROUGHOUT, BUT IT MUST ALSO TASTE OF PORK. A PORK SHOULDER COOKED WELL WILL NOT NEED MUCH ATTENTION BEFORE SERVING.

Skin the pork shoulder, reserving the skin to cure for scratchings (see page 62). Depending on the type of pork you are using, there may be a good couple of centimetres of fat under the skin. The more fat that is removed, the better the bark. Bark only occurs from the rub caramelizing on the meat. The fat, however, will produce some lovely dripping and protects the meat during cooking.

Prepare a barbecue for smoking (see The Set-Up on pages 114–15) and set the temperature to 105°C. A shoulder of pork is pretty forgiving, but keeping a constant temperature will produce the best results. Once a decent bark starts to form, the smoke no longer effectively penetrates the meat, so there is no point continuing to add more wood chunks after the first few hours of cooking.

Evenly massage the meat with 200g of the house rub and shake off any excess. Then smoke it on the barbecue, making sure it is fat (skin) side up. It can take up to 16 hours but can be ready any time after 14 hours, so keep an eye on it and have your meat probe to hand. Cooking times can vary massively — some pork just takes longer than others. The internal temperature should reach 88–90°C. Once it hits this temperature, the butt will have a thick bark and be very dark. It will not be burnt, and will not taste burnt, so don't panic. The blade bone should pull out with little resistance and the shoulder should fall in on itself if pressed gently from above. At this stage remove the pork and set aside to rest, wrapped in foil, for 30 minutes.

Unwrap the pork and turn it upside down so that the spinal bones are facing upwards. Carefully remove the spinal and rib bones from the underside of the shoulder. The small bones are very sharp, so be scrupulous. The meat around these bones is particularly special, so dig deep and work between the bones to find all you can. Remove the blade bone and the piece of tough cartilage that sits at the tip.

Start to work the meat and pull it apart. A correctly cooked shoulder should not take much work. An over-pulled shoulder will be mushy, so keep it in big chunks and strands. Add the remaining rub to taste, sprinkling it evenly like seasoning. Add the mother sauce and work this all through the meat. Check for seasoning, adding pepper and sea salt to taste. Serve immediately, in warm Potato Rolls (see page 240), with pickles (see pages 190–7), scratchings and slaws (see pages 198–203).

BARBECUE MAYO

PULLED PORK BUN

THIS IS USED AS A CONDIMENT AS
WELL AS AN INGREDIENT IN OUR BUNS,
TO STOP THE BREAD SOAKING UP TOO
MUCH MOISTURE FROM THE FILLING.

YOU WILL NEED TO ASSUME THE
TONY SOPRANO SANDWICH STANCE WHEN
YOU FINALLY ATTACK THIS. YOUR FEET
SHOULD BE SET WIDE APART SO THAT
YOU CAN GET A GOOD STABLE LEAN ON
A COUNTER TOP, WITH ELBOWS AS YOUR
RESTING POINTS. THIS TECHNIQUE WILL
SAVE YOU SHIRTS AND EMBARRASSMENT.
WHEN SIMON FIRST CAME DOWN TO THE
TRAILER, HE MADE THE MISTAKE OF
EATING HIS PULLED PORK BUN WITH A
STRAIGHT BACK AS WELL AS WEARING
A WHITE SHIRT. BAD MOVE.

MAKES 400g

Pitt Cue Barbecue Sauce *(see page 122)*	200ml
mayonnaise	200g

Simply put both the ingredients into a
bowl and mix together. Chill in the fridge
until needed.

SERVES 4

Potato Rolls or London Bath Buns *(see page 240)*	4
Barbecue Mayo *(see above)*	60ml
Hot Sauce *(see page 124)*	20ml
Pulled Pork Shoulder *(see page 135)*	600g
Mother Sauce *(see page 120)*	40ml
Bread & Butter Pickles *(see page 191)*	120g
Vinegar Slaw *(see page 203)*	120g

Slice each roll in half and lightly grill
the cut sides.

Spread the barbecue mayo on the base of
each roll and spread the hot sauce evenly
across the lid. Top each bun base with
hot pulled pork and brush lightly with the
hot mother sauce. Top with pickles and the
vinegar slaw. Put the lids on the rolls and
serve immediately.

THE TRAILER TRASH

WHEN AN UNUSED BATCH OF MACARONI WAS DEEP-FRIED IN THE RESTAURANT FOR STAFF LUNCH ONE DAY, WE THOUGHT THE KITCHEN MIGHT JUST HAVE HAD PARTICULARLY AGGRESSIVE HANGOVERS THAT REQUIRED DEEP-FRIED MEDICINE. THIS IS A VERY TRASHY BUN THAT WAS A FIXTURE ON THE TRAILER MENU, HENCE THE AFFECTIONATE NAME.

SERVES 4

leftover Hog Mac 'n' Cheese	
(see page 235), chilled	400g
plain flour	40g
House Rub (see page 119)	40g
free-range eggs	4
Japanese panko breadcrumbs	120g
oil, for deep-frying	
Potato Rolls or London Bath Buns	
(see page 240)	4
Barbecue Mayo (see page 136)	40ml
Hot Sauce (see page 124)	40ml
Pulled Pork Shoulder (see page 135)	200g
Bread & Butter Pickles (see page 191)	80g

Take your leftover chilled mac 'n' cheese and cut out four bun-sized discs.

Get ready three shallow bowls. In the first, mix the flour with the house rub, in the second beat the eggs with the milk, and in the third put the panko breadcrumbs. Lightly coat the mac 'n' cheese discs with flour, then dip them into the egg and milk mixture, and finally roll them gently in the panko breadcrumbs. Do this twice, then put them back into the fridge until needed.

Heat the oil to 180°C in a deep-fryer or large saucepan and deep-fry the mac 'n' cheese burgers for 1 minute, or until golden. Remove from the fryer and drain on kitchen paper.

To assemble, slice each roll in half. Spread the barbecue mayo on the base of each roll and the hot sauce across the lid. Place a mac 'n' cheese patty on the base of each bun and top with the pulled pork and pickles. Put the lids on and serve.

HOUSE SAUSAGE

MAKES 1 ÜBER SAUSAGE

pork shoulder	750g
pork belly	250g
pork fat	125g
beef flank or belly	125g
onions	25g
mixed peppers	250g
freshly ground black pepper	10g
smoked paprika	10g
Maldon sea salt	25g
ground coriander	10g
chilli flakes	10g
Pitt Cue Barbecue Sauce *(see page 122)*	200ml

Before you start, chill your largest mincer attachment.

Dice all the meats and put them into a bowl. Finely dice the onions and mixed peppers, discarding the seeds from the latter, and add them to the meat with all the other ingredients except the barbecue sauce. Refrigerate for 1 hour.

Remove from the fridge and put everything through the chilled mincer attachment on the largest die. Make sure the mince is thoroughly combined, then refrigerate for another hour.

Lay out strips of double-thickness clingfilm large enough to take the mince in a giant sausage, roughly 10cm thick. Roll the chilled sausage mixture in the clingfilm, place in a container of water and return it to the fridge for at least 1 hour, preferably 2, to chill and set evenly.

Prepare a barbecue for smoking (see The Set-Up on pages 114–15) and set the temperature to 180°C.

WE DEVELOPED THIS SAUSAGE AFTER A TRIP TO THE KANSAS ROYAL BARBECUE CHAMPIONSHIPS. THERE ARE LOTS OF THINGS YOU EXPECT TO LEARN FROM A HARDCORE TWO-WEEK EATING MISSION IN NEW YORK, KENTUCKY, TENNESSEE, KANSAS AND A THREE-DAY BARBECUE CHAMPIONSHIP, ESPECIALLY WHEN HANGING OUT WITH ONE OF THE TEAMS, BUT WE DIDN'T EXPECT A SAUSAGE TO BE THE THING THAT REALLY STOOD OUT. WE THOUGHT US BRITS, AND EUROPEANS AS A WHOLE, WERE THE KINGS OF SAUSAGE, BUT CLEARLY NOT. WHAT WE ATE AND SAW WAS NOT A SAUSAGE AS WE KNOW IT BUT A MASSIVE LOG OF A THING, A KIND OF MEATLOAF, UNDENIABLY PHALLIC, WHICH WAS SMOKED, LATHERED IN BARBECUE SAUCE AND SLICED INTO THICK DISCS, SIMILAR TO A COTECHINO SAUSAGE. SIMPLY AWESOME.

Remove the clingfilm from the sausage and place it on a metal tray that will fit inside your barbecue. Smoke in the barbecue to allow it to firm up a little — after 10 minutes, brush the sausage with barbecue sauce, then turn it over and brush again. After a further 10 minutes, remove it from the smoker and discard the tray.

Lower the barbecue temperature to 110°C, then place the giant sausage directly on to the grill for a further 30–45 minutes, brushing with barbecue sauce every 15 minutes until cooked right through — the internal temperature should reach 70°C when ready. Once cooked, slice into 2cm rounds and serve, or slice and chill to be grilled at a later date.

SAUSAGE BUN

SERVES 4

Potato Rolls or London Bath Buns *(see page 240)*	4
Barbecue Mayo *(see page 136)*	40ml
Hot Sauce *(see page 124)*	40ml
House Sausage slices *(see opposite)*	8
Mother Sauce *(see page 120)* or Pitt Cue Barbecue Sauce *(see page 122)*	80ml
Bread & Butter Pickles *(see page 191)*	
Green Chilli Slaw *(see page 203)*	

Slice each roll in half and lightly grill the cut sides. Spread the mayo over the base of each roll and the hot sauce across the lid.

If the sausage slices are cold, grill them for 1 minute each side.

Top each bun base with a hot sausage slice and brush the sausage with hot mother sauce. Add pickles, slaw, another sausage slice and brush with more hot sauce. Finish with more pickles and slaw, put the lids on, and serve.

THE BIG ODE

THE BIG ODE IS AFFECTIONATELY NAMED AFTER ONE OF OUR CORNISH SUPPLIERS. THIS BUN OFFERS UP A LITTLE BIT OF EVERYTHING. IT IS WORTH NOTING THAT THERE ARE NOT MANY PEOPLE BLESSED WITH A MOUTH BIG ENOUGH TO ACTUALLY EAT THIS BUN IN ANY RESPECTABLE MANNER.

SERVES 4

Potato Rolls or London Bath Buns *(see page 240)*	4
Barbecue Mayo *(see page 136)*	20ml
Pulled Pork Shoulder *(see page 135)*	80g
House Sausage slices *(see page 140)*	4
Devil Dip Gravy *(see page 130)*	20ml
Pitt Cue Burnt Ends *(see page 158)*	80g
Vinegar Slaw *(see page 203)*	
Bread & Butter Pickles *(see page 191)*	
Hot Sauce *(see page 124)*	

Slice each roll into three horizontally and grill the cut sides.

Spread the barbecue mayo on the base of each roll, and top with the pulled pork followed by a hot sausage slice. Dip the middle slice of roll in the devil dip gravy and place this on top of the sausage slice.

Next up are the burnt ends, followed by the slaw, pickles and hot sauce and finally the lids.

PITT CUE BACON

WE GO THROUGH BACON AT AN ALARMING RATE IN THE RESTAURANT, SO A BELLY MAY ONLY LAST US A FEW DAYS, BUT AT HOME IT MIGHT BE WORTH CUTTING IT INTO SMALLER SECTIONS AND FREEZING IT AFTER HANGING.

MAKES 5KG

black peppercorns	25g
fennel seeds	25g
muscovado sugar	100g
Maldon sea salt	350g
beautifully fat pork belly, skin removed	1, weighing 5kg

Toast the peppercorns and fennel seeds in a dry frying pan for a few minutes, shaking the pan, until golden. Remove from the heat and grind to a powder with a mortar and pestle, then combine with the sugar and salt. Rub this dry cure mixture all over the pork belly, then wrap it tightly in clingfilm. Place the wrapped belly in the fridge and leave to cure for 5 days.

When ready, rinse off the dry cure mixture (it will be very wet by now) and leave to dry in the fridge overnight.

At this point the bacon can be wrapped in muslin to hang in a very cool space, or, if your fridge allows it, it can be hung naked in the fridge until it reaches your desired level of maturity. The bacon will mature more quickly outside the fridge and can be brought into the fridge when ready. The longer it hangs, the stiffer, more intense and more salty the bacon will be. We hang our bacon for 2—3 weeks in the fridge.

— DEVILLED PIGS' FEET —

WHEN ONE OF THE MOST IMPORTANT PARTS OF THE PIG MEETS A SUPER SEXY
GRAVY THERE IS NOT MUCH YOU CANNOT ACHIEVE. TROTTERS ARE GIVEN A LOT OF
ATTENTION AT PITT CUE. THEY ARE SMOKED FOR THEIR DRIPPING AND STOCKPILED
FOR ALL THE SAUCES. THIS RECIPE IS SOMETHING OF A 'MASTER RECIPE',
TO BE MADE IN BULK AND CHIPPED AWAY AT WHENEVER A SAUCE OR DISH
IS LACKING AND NEEDS A KICK UP THE BUM.

MAKES APPROXIMATELY 1 LITRE

pigs' feet, as long as possible	4
Master Chicken Brine (see page 90)	500ml
onion, peeled	1
carrot, peeled	1
stick of celery	1
leek	1
bulb of garlic	½
mixed herbs (thyme, rosemary, bay, parsley)	bunch
Devil Dip Gravy (see page 130), without mustard or butter	500ml

Shave the pigs' feet using a disposable
razor, and singe any remaining hair over
an open flame. Wash the feet thoroughly,
then put them into a plastic container
and cover with the master chicken brine.
Refrigerate overnight.

Prepare a barbecue for smoking (see The Set-Up
on pages 114–15) and set the temperature
to 120°C. Alternatively, heat your oven to
120°C/250°F/gas mark ¼.

Drain the pigs' feet and place them in a
casserole that will fit inside your barbecue,
if using. Cover with cold water and bring to
the boil, then drain, discarding the water.
Put the pigs' feet back into the casserole
with the vegetables and herbs and cover with
the devil dip gravy. Half cover with a lid
and either smoke in the barbecue or cook in
the oven for 6 hours or overnight.

When cooked, drain the sauce through a fine
sieve into a large pan and reserve. Allow
the pigs' feet to cool, then pick all the
fat, meat and skin off them, add to the
sauce and bring to the boil.

Pack into sterilized jars (see page 78) and
seal. When cool, refrigerate until needed.

BELLY CHOPS

A WHOLE PORK BELLY IS A SUCH EXCITING OPTION AND AN INCREDIBLY VERSATILE
CUT. COOKED THIS WAY, THE BELLY GIVES YOU ALL THE ENJOYMENT OF THE RIB,
ALBEIT IN LARGER CHOP FORM, WITH THE THE ADDED BONUS OF THE QUIVERING
FATTY GOODNESS THAT IS TRIMMED FROM THE BELLY WHEN CUTTING SPARE RIBS.
IF YOU FIND A BELLY THAT HAS BEEN HUNG FOR A WEEK OR SO WITH HARD DRY SKIN,
ALL THE BETTER AS THIS WILL AID ANY EXTRA-CURRICULAR CRACKLING PURSUITS.
WE SERVE OUR BELLY CHOPS, MOST OFTEN FROM TAMWORTHS, WITH APPLE KETCHUP
TO CUT THE RICHNESS AND SOME PUFFED PIG'S SKIN.

SERVES 4

thick end belly, skin removed	1.5kg
long sprig of rosemary	1

SPICES

cumin seeds	1 tsp
celery seeds	1 tsp
chilli flakes	1 tsp
star anise	1 tsp
smoked paprika	1 tsp
coriander seeds	1 tsp
mustard seeds	1 tsp
fennel seeds	20g
black peppercorns	20g

MARINADE

ground spices (see above)	75g
vegetable oil	100ml
Tabasco	100ml
English mustard	100g
Maldon sea salt	100g
cider	100ml
maple syrup	100g
blackstrap molasses	100ml
apricot preserve	100g

Heat the oven to 180°C/350°F/gas mark 4.
Put all the spices into a roasting tin and
roast for 10 minutes, or until golden.
Put into a blender and blitz to a powder.

Put all the marinade ingredients into a
bowl and mix together. Remove the skin
from the ribs and add to the marinade.
Massage the ribs well with the marinade and
refrigerate overnight.

Prepare a barbecue for smoking (see The Set-Up
on pages 114—15) and set the temperature
to 105°C.

Remove the ribs from the fridge and shake
off the excess marinade. Do not discard the
marinade. Put the ribs, bone side down, on
your barbecue and smoke them for 6—7 hours,
until they reach an internal temperature
of 85—87°C. Test them by holding them with
tongs to see if they bounce — if they have
a bit of resistance, similar to the touch
of a medium-rare steak, they are ready.

Cut the ribs into portions. Put the reserved
marinade into a pan and simmer until it has
reduced slightly. Baste the ribs liberally
with the reduced marinade, then allow to
cool and set aside.

To finish, adjust your barbecue for direct
grilling (see page 112) and grill the ribs
for 2 minutes on each side, using the
rosemary sprig as a brush to baste the meat
with the reduced marinade as it cooks.

PORK RIBS

SERVES 2

rack of pork spare ribs	1
House Rub *(see page 119)*	70g
Mother Sauce *(see page 120)*	100ml

Remove the membrane on the back of the ribs. Kitchen paper is the best thing to use for this. Get a blunt knife and carefully prise back the membrane from the tips of the first rib bone. Hold the membrane with the kitchen paper and it should pull back completely with a little force. Think skinning a flat fish. The spare rib rack can be cooked as is, but if the rack is squared up to a St Louis-style cut, you will be left with the rib tips to play with.

Remove the last four small ribs from the thin end of the rack and trim the rack into a neat, compact rectangle. This will require a section called the 'rib tips' to be removed from the base of the rack. The rack will cook more evenly like this. If this seems like too much work, then cooking the rack as spare ribs is absolutely fine. Keep the tips and trim aside.

Prepare a barbecue for smoking (see The Set-Up on pages 114–15) and set the temperature to 105°C.

Coat the rack all over with the rub and shake off any excess. Lay the rack, bone side down, on the barbecue and smoke for up to 6 hours, checking after 4 hours to see how the ribs are getting on. When the internal temperature reaches 86°C, you can

EVERYONE LOVES A GOOD RIB. JUST AS A CHICKEN SHOULD HAVE BEEN CREATED WITH MORE WINGS, SO SHOULD A PIG HAVE BEEN CREATED WITH MORE BELLY.

WE LIKE OUR RIBS SIMPLE, WITH JUST A TOUCH OF OUR MOTHER SAUCE TO FINISH THEM OFF. THIS RECIPE IS AS SIMPLE AS WE CAN MAKE IT AND WILL PROVIDE GREAT RIBS TO BE EATEN AT HOME. START SIMPLE, THEN EVOLVE AND TRY NEW THINGS ONCE YOU ARE SATISFIED THAT THE BASICS ARE NAILED.

start to apply the mother sauce.

The ribs can be removed at 86–90°C. They should have a bit of resistance, similar to the feeling of a medium-rare steak, and the surface of the bark should begin to crack when bounced with tongs. Remove from the grill and leave to rest in foil.

Adjust the barbecue for direct grilling over a high heat (see page 112). At this stage you can either portion the ribs individually or grill the rack whole. Grill the rack or ribs for 1–2 minutes on each side. Paint liberally with mother sauce, then serve immediately. We like to add a small dusting of rub when serving – Smoked Bacon Rub (see page 119) would be a very good idea.

PORK CHUCK

THIS IS A BRILLIANT JOINT FROM THE SHOULDER AND MAY JUST BE OUR FAVOURITE AMONG THOSE FOUND ON A PIG. IT IS ALSO A GREAT CUT TO SEARCH OUT IF YOU FANCY SOME LAMB OR MUTTON. THE CHOPS FROM THE SHOULDER HAVE JUST ABOUT THE PERFECT RATIO OF MUSCLE TO FAT, WITH MUCH THE SAME SOFTNESS IN THE MUSCLE AS THE BEST END OF THE LOIN TO WHICH THEY JOIN, BUT ARE AN ALL-ROUND MORE FLAVOURSOME PROPOSITION. THE SHOULDER USUALLY PROVIDES SIX OR SEVEN 300G CHOPS, DEPENDING ON THE BREED AND SIZE OF PIG, AND AT THE RESTAURANT WE BREAK IT DOWN IN TWO WAYS: INTO CHOPS, OR INTO TWO LARGER JOINTS THAT EQUATE TO THREE CHOPS EACH. THESE TWO LARGER JOINTS FROM THE SHOULDER MAKE A PERFECT SHARING PLATE AND ARE LARGE ENOUGH TO BE SMOKED SLOWLY TO MEDIUM-RARE BEFORE BEING FINISHED ON THE GRILL.

SERVES 4

pork chuck, on the bone	1, weighing 1kg
Maldon sea salt	
freshly ground black pepper	

Prepare a barbecue for smoking (see The Set-Up on pages 114–15) and set the temperature to 110°C.

Season the chuck all over with pepper and place in your barbecue. Smoke for 45 minutes– 1 hour, until the internal temperature reaches 52–55°C, then remove from the smoker, wrap in clingfilm and set aside to rest.

Meanwhile, adjust the barbecue for direct grilling (see page 112). When the grill is hot, season the chuck with lots of salt and grill for 1–2 minutes on each side so that the meat browns evenly. Remove from the grill and leave to rest for 10 minutes before carving.

To carve, take the meat off the bone and carve against the grain. Season between the slices and serve, not forgetting the resting juices from the chopping board or that would be a grave sin. Serve with Fruit Ketchups (see pages 126–7).

PITT CUE PORK CHOP

SERVES 1

best end pork chop or shoulder chop   1, weighing 350g
smoked Maldon sea salt
freshly ground black pepper

We'd like to assume that you are using a
beautiful piece of pork that has 2—3cm of fat
between the skin and the first sign of meat.
Remove the skin from the chop and set aside.
Try to leave a good 2cm of fat running along
the top of the loin.

Set your barbecue for medium-hot direct
grilling (see page 112) and allow it to cool
slightly, with white embers. This is our
favourite time to cook a pork chop.

Season the chop with the sea salt and pepper
on both sides and place it on the barbecue.
Listen to it crackle and pop for a minute.
This is perhaps the most comforting sound
ever. Cook the chop for 10 minutes, moving
it every 20—30 seconds to another part
of the grill and turning regularly — this
will help cook the chop evenly. The surface
should be a deep caramel when cooked, with
intermittent charring.

Turn the chop on to its edge on the coolest
part of the grill and allow the fat to cook
for 2 minutes. Be vigilant for flare-ups.
Using a probe, aim for an internal
temperature of 53°C. When you reach this
will be dependent on the heat of the grill.
Remove the chop from the grill and leave
to rest for 10 minutes on a board, turning
occasionally. This will produce a chop that
is blushing pink all the way through.

THIS IS ABOUT AS SIMPLE
A RECIPE AS ONE CAN FIND
BUT IT IS VERY EASY TO GET
IT WRONG, STARTING FROM THE
WRONG PORK RIGHT THROUGH
TO THE MISMANAGEMENT OF
THE GRILL WHEN COOKING THE
CHOP. ONCE YOU SOURCE, COOK
AND EAT A VERY AWESOME PORK
CHOP, THERE ARE FEW THINGS
THAT WILL BRING AS MUCH
SATISFACTION.

Working along the bone, remove the loin
and cut into 1cm slices across the chop.
Season with salt and pepper between the
slices and arrange the slices back on
the bone of the loin.

Pick up any resting juices from the chopping
board by scraping the flat blade of your
knife across the board and pour them over
the chop. Eat immediately, with a big blob
of Apple Ketchup (see page 126), and feel
exceptionally good about life.

— HOT GUTS —

THE 'HOT GUT' ORIGINATED
FROM SOUTHSIDE MARKET IN
ELGIN, TEXAS, IN 1886.
SADLY, THE HOT GUTS OF TODAY
ARE TAMER AND LEANER THAN
THOSE OF YORE. THEY'RE STILL
QUITE GOOD, THOUGH.

MAKES APPROXIMATELY 40 SAUSAGES

natural lamb's runners, for the casings	
aged beef flank, chilled	1kg
aged beef shoulder, chilled	1kg
beef fat, chilled	250g
bone marrow, chilled	250g
breadcrumbs	250g
beer, chilled	250ml
freshly ground black pepper	20g
smoked chipotle Tabasco	30ml
hot mustard	30g
light muscovado sugar	25g
garlic cloves, chopped	10g
smoked Maldon sea salt	50g
thyme leaves	1 tsp

Thoroughly soak and rinse the lamb's runners before using — make sure to rinse through the middle as well as the outside.

Dice the meat, fat and bone marrow into 2cm cubes. Place in a chilled bowl and mix together with the remaining ingredients. Feed the mixture through a coarse 8mm mincer attachment into another chilled bowl.

Beat the mixture for 5 minutes until well bound, then load your sausage stuffer (or use a sausage stuffing attachment on your mincer) and stuff the mixture into the casings. Tie off the sausages as best you can. The sausages are now ready to be cooked, but we suggest to hang them in your fridge for a few days first, as this will aid the cooking process.

PORGER SAUSAGE

THIS IS THE GRANDDADDY OF SAUSAGES,
SUPER COMPLEX AND MEATY, OFFERING
ALL THE JUICINESS OF A RARE BREED
PORK SAUSAGE, WITH SMOKY PORKINESS
FROM THE BACON AND AN UNDERLYING
NUTTINESS FROM WELL-AGED BEEF. MAKE
SURE YOU USE DRY-AGED BEEF, 30—45
DAYS HUNG, AND TOP-QUALITY PORK IN
THIS RECIPE, AS IT REALLY MAKES ALL
THE DIFFERENCE.

MAKES APPROXIMATELY 25 SAUSAGES

natural lamb's runners, for the casings	
fat belly pork, chilled	500g
shoulder of pork, chilled	500g
dry-aged beef rib cap, chilled	500g
dry-aged beef rib-eye end of chuck, chilled	500g
smoked streaky bacon, rind removed, chilled	500g
salt	40g
ground white pepper	10g
water	200ml
garlic cloves, peeled and crushed	3-4
fennel seeds, toasted and ground	1 tsp

Thoroughly soak and rinse the lamb's runners before using — make sure to rinse through the middle as well as the outside.

Dice all the meat into 2cm cubes, place in a chilled bowl and mix together with the remaining ingredients. Feed the mixture through a coarse 8mm mincer attachment into another chilled bowl.

Beat the mixture for 5 minutes until well bound, then feed the mixture through a 5mm mincer attachment. Load your sausage stuffer (or use a sausage stuffing attachment on your mincer) and stuff the mixture into the casings. Tie off the sausages as best you can. The sausages are now ready to be cooked, but we suggest to hang them in your fridge for a few days first, as this will aid the cooking process.

PITT CUE
SMOKED BRISKET

EASY TO GET WRONG BUT UNBELIEVABLE WHEN COOKED PERFECTLY, BRISKET IS
LARGELY A LEAN MUSCLE THAT CAN DRY OUT WHEN COOKED, LACKING THE FAT
THAT AIDS OTHER CUTS OF BEEF. THE QUALITY OF THE BEEF IS VITAL HERE,
AND IT TOOK AN AGE TO FINALLY FIND THE RIGHT BEEF SO THAT WE COULD
GET BRISKET ON THE MENU. IT'S A STAPLE IN TEXAS AND REVERED THROUGHOUT
THE SOUTHERN STATES OF THE US.

GOOD BRISKET SHOULD HAVE 4–5 WEEKS HANGING ON THE BONE, THEN ANOTHER WEEK
OFF THE BONE. WE TAKE THE LARGER, OLDER ANIMALS THAT HAVE A LARGER POINT
END AND HAVE HAD TIME TO DEVELOP FLAVOUR AND INTRAMUSCULAR FAT. TRUST
YOUR BUTCHER AND SEE WHAT THEY CAN DO. THE POINT END IS BASICALLY HALF A
BRISKET, CUT STRAIGHT ACROSS THE MIDDLE WHERE THE FATTY POINT MUSCLE THAT
SITS ON THE LEAN 'FLAT' MUSCLE STOPS. THE CUT COMPRISES OF ROUGHLY
70 PER CENT POINT, 30 PER CENT LEAN FLAT MUSCLE.

SERVES 8

brisket, point end cut (see above)	3–4kg
Beef Rub (see page 119)	75g

Prepare a barbecue for smoking (see The
Set-Up on pages 114–15) and set the
temperature to 115°C.

Coat the brisket all over with the house
rub, then place it, point side up, in your
barbecue. There is a fine line between
perfectly cooked brisket and overcooked
brisket, so putting a digital thermometer
in the meat is very helpful. Smoke the
brisket until the internal temperature
reaches 86–88°C. This can take anything from
12 to 13 hours, depending on the beef used.

When the beef reaches 86–88°C, give it a
prod. It should have a somewhat sexy wobble.
The sexy wobble is key. Remove the beef
from the barbecue and wrap it in clingfilm
and foil to rest.

To serve the brisket there are a couple
of options. The cut contains two separate
muscles, the flat and the point. These
muscles run in different directions —
roughly 45 degrees from each other. If you
don't mind having a slice where the two
muscles are running differently, slice
them together.

We prefer to separate the muscles. They
can simply be pulled away gently from one
another by working your knife, or fingers,
between them. The fat will be so soft that
it requires little effort. Be careful — it
will be very hot. Once separated, trim any
excess fat, but do not remove it entirely,
as it is this fat that brings so much joy
to the eating. Now slice against the grain
of both the flat and the point. You can also
slice the point into 2cm slabs, then finish
both sides by direct grilling on a barbecue
(see page 112), painting them repeatedly
with Mother Sauce (see page 120) or Devil
Dip Gravy (see page 130). The fatty brisket
point also browns incredibly well in a hot
pan and brings another level of flavour to
the brisket.

PITT CUE BURNT ENDS

OUR LOVE AFFAIR WITH BRISKET RUNS DEEP, AND BURNT ENDS ARE OUR REAL GUILTY PLEASURE. WHEN THIS IS ON THE MENU WE'LL CONSTANTLY FIND OURSELVES WITH A PIECE OF GRILLED BREAD IN THE KITCHEN, HUNTING DOWN THE PAN WHERE WE ARE COOKING OUR SMOKED BRISKET. IF YOU IGNORE THE UNWRITTEN RULEBOOK, HOWEVER, THIS RECIPE CAN BE A GREAT WAY OF SAVING THE OCCASIONAL BRISKET THAT DOESN'T COME OUT QUITE RIGHT (AND WHEN COOKING BRISKET FOR THE FIRST TIME, THERE WILL BE A FEW OF THESE). DON'T BE AFRAID TO USE A WHOLE BRISKET, FLAT AND POINT. ENTHUSIASTS MAY SAY IT'S NOT 'BURNT ENDS', BUT HEY HO, YOU CAN'T PLEASE EVERYONE. GREAT BEEF SHOULD HAVE STUNNINGLY TASTY FAT AND THE MORE AVAILABLE THE BETTER, IN OUR OPINION. THE PURISTS MAY DISAGREE … BUT WE ARE NOT PURISTS. WE LOVE THIS RECIPE SO MUCH, WE ADD IT TO EVERYTHING. IT DOMINATES OUR BRISKET BUNS AND MAKES MASH EPIC. IT MAKES A FINE CROQUETTE, A WORTHY NUGGET, EVEN BAO ACCORDING TO ONE CUSTOMER, AND CAN PLAY ITS PART IN A COTTAGE PIE.

SERVES 4–6

Pitt Cue Smoked Brisket (see page 156)	1kg
Mother Sauce (see page 120)	300ml
Pitt Cue Barbecue Sauce (see page 122)	300ml

Prepare a barbecue for smoking (see The Set-Up on pages 114–15) and set the temperature to 120°C.

Cut the brisket, flat and as much point end as you wish to use for your burnt ends, into rough 2–3cm square dice. Heat a flameproof pan that will fit inside your barbecue, add the diced brisket and cook for 10 minutes, stirring occasionally, until evenly browned. There should be a lovely smell of well-browned beef. Add the mother sauce and barbecue sauce and cook for a further 15 minutes. Transfer the pan to the barbecue and smoke for 30 minutes, then serve.

Store the burnt ends in the fridge — they keep well and can be reheated when needed.

BRISKET BUNS

THE ONLY THING THAT MIGHT
MAKE THESE BUNS BETTER IS
CHEESE. HEAT SOME OGLESHIELD,
OR OTHER AWESOME CHEDDAR,
THROUGH THE BURNT ENDS FOR
ADDED ENJOYMENT.

SERVES 4

Potato Rolls *(see page 240)*	4
Barbecue Mayo *(see page 136)*	20ml
Hot Sauce *(see page 124)*	40ml
Pitt Cue Burnt Ends *(see opposite)*	200g
Pitt Cue Smoked Brisket, sliced *(see page 156)*	400g
Mother Sauce *(see page 120)*	
or Devil Dip Gravy *(see page 130)*	60ml
Bread & Butter Pickles *(see page 191)*	80g
Vinegar Slaw *(see page 203)*	80g

Slice each roll in half and lightly grill
each the sides. Spread the barbecue mayo
on the base of each roll and the hot sauce
across the lids.

Top each bun base with the sliced brisket
and add the burnt ends on top. Spread the
brisket with warm mother sauce or devil dip
gravy. Top with the pickles and slaw.
Put the lids on and serve immediately.

SLOW-GRILLED
————— DENVER CUT —————

SERVES 4

Beef Denver cut	1, weighing 1.5-2kg
Beef Rub *(see page 118)*	50g
smoked Maldon sea salt	
freshly ground black pepper	

Prepare a barbecue for smoking (see The Set-Up on pages 114–15) and set the temperature to 110°C.

Rub the chuck all over with the beef rub and place in the barbecue to smoke for about 45 minutes, or until the internal temperature of the meat reaches 48°C on your meat probe.

As soon as the beef reaches temperature, remove it from the barbecue, wrap in clingfilm and leave to rest for 10 minutes while you adjust the barbecue for direct grilling (see page 112). At this point the whole cut can be grilled and carved, or cut into smaller steaks, as we do in the restaurant, and grilled individually.

When the barbecue is hot, season the beef with salt and pepper and place on the grill. Grill the beef for 2 minutes, turning every 20 seconds or so. Remove from the grill and leave to rest for 7–10 minutes. To serve, carve against the grain into thin slices with a sharp knife, as you would a steak, and serve immediately with an Iceberg Salad (see page 210) and perhaps some Pumpkin Home Fries (see page 232).

BEEF CHUCK USUALLY GETS MINCED FOR BURGERS OR CUT INTO CHUCK STEAKS, SO CALL YOUR BUTCHER AND ASK HIM TO RESERVE THIS CUT FOR YOU.

JUST AS PORK SHOULDER IS A WONDERFUL CUT TO SLOWLY COOK TO MEDIUM OR MEDIUM-RARE, SO IS ITS BEEF COUNTERPART. THE DENVER CUT IS ONE OF THE MANY MUSCLES THAT MAKE UP THE CHUCK AND SITS ON TOP OF THE EYE OF LOIN AS IT ENTERS THE SHOULDER. AS WITH ALL CUTS THAT ARE SMOKED TO MEDIUM-RARE OR RARE BEFORE GRILLING, THE LEVEL OF SMOKE IN THE BARBECUE NEEDS TO BE MONITORED, AS TOO MUCH SMOKE CAN QUICKLY RUIN YOUR MEAT AND YOUR DAY.

FEATHERBLADE

THE FEATHERBLADE COMES FROM THE SHOULDER OF THE BEAST AND IS THE
FLAT MUSCLE THAT SITS ON THE BLADE BONE ITSELF. IT HAS A THICK BIT
OF TENDON THAT RUNS THROUGH THE CENTRE WHICH SEPARATES WHAT IS OFTEN
KNOWN AS THE FLAT IRON STEAKS. THE STRONG GRAIN ALONG EACH SIDE OF THE
CENTRAL TENDON CREATES A FEATHERED EFFECT ALONG THE SIDE OF THE CUT.
IT IS A FANTASTIC CUT WITH THE ADDED BONUS THAT IT CAN BE LEFT ON THE
BLADE BONE TO DRY-AGE. ANY GOOD BUTCHER SHOULD HAVE NO PROBLEM RESERVING
THIS CUT FOR YOU. FEATHERBLADE MAY WELL COME WITH A THICK LAYER OF
HARD FAT ON TOP. TRIM THIS TO 5MM—1CM THICK. THE BETTER THE BEEF WE CAN
SOURCE, THE MORE INCLINED WE ARE TO LEAVE MORE OF THE FAT ON.

THIS DISH CAN BE COOKED ON OR OFF THE BONE. ON THE BONE WILL
REQUIRE A FURTHER 30—45 MINUTES COOKING AT LEAST, AND MAKES FOR A
PREHISTORIC SERVING OPTION.

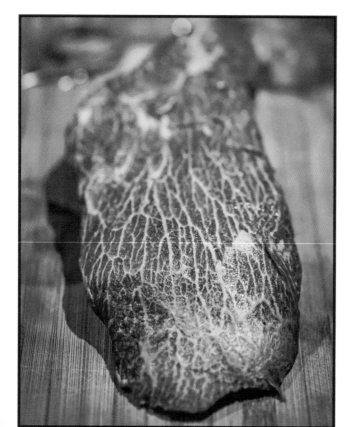

SERVES 4—6

dry-aged beef featherblade	1, weighing about 1.5kg
Beef Rub (see page 118)	100g
Pickled Shiitake (see page 89), to serve	

Prepare a barbecue for smoking (see The Set-Up on pages 114—15) and set the temperature to 110°C.

Cover the featherblade evenly with the beef rub and shake off any excess. Place the featherblade, fat side up, in your barbecue and smoke for 10—12 hours. The internal temperature should reach 87°C when cooked and the meat should be slightly soft to the touch, similar to a well-cooked brisket. If you are unsure, slice off a small chunk and try it.

When ready, remove the meat from the barbecue and let it rest, wrapped in foil, for 20 minutes.

Using a very sharp knife, cut the meat into 5mm slices and arrange on a plate. You will notice the 'feather' when slicing like this. Serve the featherblade slices with pickled shiitake. This recipe is also awesome served in fresh Potato Rolls (see page 240) with some slaw (see pages 198–203).

SMOKED STANDING RIB ROAST
—— WITH DRIPPING TRENCHER ——

THE SMOKED PRIME RIB FROM SMITTY'S MARKET IN LOCKHART, TEXAS,
WAS AWESOME. THEY WENT TO THE EFFORT OF SOURCING REALLY GOOD GRASS-FED BEEF,
AND COMBINED WITH A SIMPLE RUB IT WAS, ALONGSIDE WITNESSING SOME VERY LOOSE
SHOOTING-RANGE ETIQUETTE, ONE OF THE MOST MEMORABLE THINGS ABOUT TEXAS.
WE TESTED THIS RECIPE OUT ON THE TRAILER ONE SUNDAY WITH SOME OF
OUR BEAUTIFUL BEEF FROM CORNWALL.

WE SERVE THIS JUST AS WE DO WITH MOST OF OUR STEAKS IN THE RESTAURANT,
SITTING ON TOP OF A BONE MARROW TRENCHER WITH POPOVERS AND DEVIL DIP GRAVY.
THIS IS OUR ANSWER TO A SUNDAY ROAST.

SERVES 10

Beef Rub *(see page 118)*	50g
forerib or wing rib of beef	1, weighing about 4kg

Whipped Bone Marrow, to serve *(see page 228)*
Maldon sea salt
freshly ground black pepper

Prepare a barbecue for smoking (see The Set-Up
on pages 114–15) and set the temperature to 80°C.

Rub the beef rub all over the joint, then
smoke it in the barbecue for 5 hours, or until
the internal temperature reaches 55–57°C — it
will continue to rise even after it has been
removed from the barbecue, to around 59°C.

Once the rib reaches temperature, remove it
from the barbecue and adjust the barbecue
for direct grilling at a medium heat (see
page 112).

Season the meat joint with salt and pepper,
then cook on the barbecue, turning every
minute or so, for 5–6 minutes, or until
the joint has the full Maillard effect (see
page 108). It should be evenly browned, but
not charred, and have a sweet nutty smell.
Rest for 10 minutes and serve on a Dripping
Trencher smothered in Whipped Bone Marrow
(see page 166) with Devil Dip Gravy (see
page 130) and Popovers (see page 243).

DRIPPING TRENCHER

IT IS NICE TO THINK THAT MEDIEVAL DINING STILL HAS A PLACE ON OUR TABLES. IN MEDIEVAL TIMES, FOOD WOULD OFTEN BE PLACED UPON STALE OR DENSE PIECES OF BREAD. THE BREAD, HAVING SOAKED UP THE MEAT JUICES AND SAUCE, WOULD THEN EITHER BE EATEN OR HANDED OUT TO THOSE IN NEED OF SUSTENANCE.

OUR DRIPPING TRENCHER IS THE PERFECT FOUNDATION FOR ROAST MEAT. THINK OF IT AS THE BEST MOP IN THE WORLD. WHENEVER WE PUT A RIB OR RUMP FOR SHARING ON THE MENU, WE SIT IT ON A TRENCHER SMEARED WITH A LIVELY BONE MARROW MIXTURE AND LEAVE IT TO REST FOR AS LONG AS THE TRENCHER NEEDS TO FULFIL ITS POTENTIAL.

MAKES ENOUGH FOR 1 RIB ROAST

semi-skimmed milk	200ml
water	100ml
fresh yeast	5g
strong white flour	250g
wholemeal flour	250g
beef dripping or bone marrow	100g
salt	5g
caster sugar	5g

Heat the milk and water to 35°C, then add the yeast, followed by the sifted flours and the remaining ingredients. Bring the ingredients together, then cover with a damp tea towel and leave to prove in a warm place for 20 minutes, or until it has doubled in size.

Remove the mixture from the bowl and knock back into a dough, then roll out to the size of a large plate, big enough to take your smoked standing rib roast. Place on a baking tray, cover and prove for another 20 minutes.

Heat the oven to 180°C/350°F/gas mark 4. Bake the trencher for 20 minutes, or until golden brown.

Slice off the top of the trencher and use this as a serving platter for the smoked standing rib roast, where you can leave it to rest for 10 minutes after cooking.

BEEF RIBS

THE QUALITY OF THE BEEF HERE IS EVERYTHING. IT TOOK US A YEAR BEFORE A BEEF RIB WAS EVEN SERVED AT PITT CUE. IT WAS ONLY WHEN WE SPENT TIME WITH OUR BUTCHERS IN CORNWALL THAT WE THOUGHT BEEF RIBS SHOULD HAVE A PLACE ON OUR MENU. OUR RIBS COME FROM GRASS-FED, RARE-BREED RIB-EYES THAT ARE KEPT ON THE BONE FOR AT LEAST 4 WEEKS, AND ARE HUNG FOR A FURTHER WEEK OR SO AFTER BEING REMOVED FROM THE RIB-EYE, WHICH DRIES THEM OUT A LITTLE. THE RACK, 4–6 BONES IN LENGTH, SHOULD BE STIFF, FIRM AND HAVE A DISTINCTIVE SWEET, NUTTY AROMA. TRY TO AVOID RIBS FROM THE WING RIB — THE RIBS FLATTEN OUT TOWARDS THE SIRLOIN, ARE GENERALLY CUT LONGER AND CONTAIN LESS INTERCOSTAL MEAT.

SERVES 2

4-6 bone beef rib rack	1, weighing 500-600g
House Rub (see page 119)	50g
Mother Sauce (see page 120)	
or Pitt Cue Barbecue Sauce (see page 122), (optional)	

Crucial to the eating of the beef rib is the removal of the membrane on the underside, especially with a well-aged rib. Unlike the pork rib membrane, which is fresh and thin, the membrane on the underside of the beef rib is thick and a bit of a pain. To remove it, score down each side of the individual bones, being careful not to cut into the flesh. Get a proper butcher's knife with some flexibility and work up the rib, removing the membrane with as little flesh as possible. Try to keep the knife as flat as you can to the flesh, just skinning the membrane from it. The removed membrane should be about 2cm wide and run the entire length of each rib. All that will remain is a small section of membrane on the rib bone itself, which is a fair compromise.

Cover the rack all over with the rub and shake off any excess.

Prepare a barbecue for smoking (see The Set-Up on pages 114–15) and set the temperature to 110°C, though anything up to 130°C will produce tasty beef ribs.

There is a huge amount of fat running through the intercostal muscles of the beef rib, which can take a bit of a battering through temperature rises without drying out. 110°C is ideal, but don't panic if the barbecue peaks and dips in temperature.

Smoke the rack for 5–6 hours, until the meat has pulled back from the bone. By then the rack will have the French trim effect, with the bone a little bit exposed. The internal temperature should be about 89–92°C, the meat squidgy and soft with a thick dark crust. We like the ribs naked, but if you fancy them sauced, give them a good basting with mother sauce or barbecue sauce 30 minutes before removing them. Alternatively adjust the barbecue for direct grilling (see page 112) and paint them constantly with the sauce while turning them over the heat.

The smell of a newly smoked beef rib is unbelievable. Serve immediately, with some Pickled Shiitake (see page 89) to boost that amazing umami beefiness while balancing the richness.

LAMB RIBS
── WITH MOLASSES MOP & ONION SALAD ──

LIVING NEXT TO THE BEST TURKISH OCAKBASI IN LONDON WAS BOUND TO HAVE
KNOCK-ON EFFECTS. NOT ONLY DO YOU START TO APPRECIATE ANGRY WAITERS THAT
CANNOT WAIT TO GET YOU OUT OF THE DOOR, YOU COME TO LOVE THE WAY CITRUS,
HERBS, JUST-COOKED ONIONS AND ACIDIC FRUITS CAN BENEFIT GRILLED MEAT.

THIS RECIPE IS THE CULMINATION OF TOM'S MANY SUNDAY NIGHT POST-SERVICE PIT STOPS
TO THE TURKISH SUPERMARKET, WHERE HE WOULD GRAB A FEW BOTTLES OF POMEGRANATE
MOLASSES, SOME SUMAC AND AS MANY LITTLE QUAIL AS HE COULD SAFELY CARRY ON HIS
BIKE. WHILE QUAIL, SUMAC AND BURNT ONIONS STILL HAVE A PLACE ON THE MENU AT
PITT CUE, THERE ARE FEW THINGS THAT CAN TOP LAMB RIBS WITH THIS SALAD.

SERVES 2

whole lamb belly/breast on the bone	1, weighing 600g
French's mustard	20ml
Lamb Rub *(see page 118)*	50g

MOLASSES MOP

Mother Sauce *(see page 120)*	200ml
blackstrap molasses	15ml
juice of 1 lemon	

RED ONION & BABY GEM SALAD

firm, small red onions	4
extra virgin olive oil	
baby gem lettuces	2
juice of 2 lemons	
large mint leaves	10
flat-leaf parsley leaves	small handful
pickled pomegranates	2 tbsp
pomegranate molasses	40ml
sumac	1 tbsp
Maldon sea salt	
freshly ground black pepper	

Prepare a barbecue for smoking (see The Set-Up on pages 114–15) and set the temperature to 110°C.

There is no need to remove the membrane on the lamb belly. It is very thin and doesn't really affect the eating, though the skin on the top side of the belly will need to be removed, as it will become tough and unpleasant to eat. Square off the belly and trim the redundant flap from the smaller end of the belly (rear-end). The yield of a lamb rib is never going to be great, and there is very little meat from the trim, so don't worry if it looks as though you've reduced the rack to a small rectangle. The belly should also be squared off at the shoulder end. The rack of ribs should be nice and neat.

Put all the molasses mop ingredients in a pan and bring to a simmer. Set aside and keep warm.

Rub the rack all over with the mustard and coat evenly with the lamb rub, shaking off any excess. Smoke the lamb in the barbecue for about 5 hours, or until the meat is just starting to soften and the internal temperature reaches 87°C.

Remove the ribs from the barbecue and set aside. Adjust the barbecue for direct grilling (see page 112). Grill the ribs and baste generously with the molasses mop. Remove the ribs from the grill and keep warm.

To make the salad, peel and quarter the onions and dress lightly in olive oil. Grill the onions on the barbecue for 10 minutes or until charred and softened, then remove and place in a bowl, cover with clingfilm and leave to steam. Quarter the baby gems, season with salt and pepper and brush with olive oil. Grill for 1 minute on each side, or until the baby gems are sporadically dark and charred but not completely burnt. Remove from the grill and set aside.

Lightly peel off most of the burnt outer layer from the onions to leave the lightly charred and soft inner layers, then combine with the baby gems. Dress with a tablespoon of olive oil, the lemon juice, torn mint leaves, parsley leaves, pickled pomegranates and pomegranate molasses. Toss the whole salad gently until well combined and evenly dressed. Season to taste with salt, some sumac and freshly ground black pepper.

Serve the ribs sprinkled with the remaining sumac and alongside a nice heap of the grilled onion salad.

LAMB RUMP

LAMB RUMP IS A WICKED LITTLE JOINT FOR THE BARBECUE, COMPACT, EASILY PORTIONABLE AND YET ANOTHER CUT THAT SUITS A COMBINATION OF INDIRECT AND DIRECT COOKING. YOU WANT A RUMP WITH A PROPER COVERING OF FAT (USE HOGGET OR MUTTON, IF YOU CAN FIND IT) THAT WILL CHAR AND DEVELOP ALL THOSE COMPLEX SWEET AND SMOKY FLAVOURS THAT MAKE GOOD ANIMAL FATS SO RIDICULOUSLY ADDICTIVE WHEN FINISHED ON THE GRILL. YOUR BUTCHER WILL PROBABLY OFFER TO TRIM THE JOINT, WHICH MEANS REMOVING THE THICK END OF THE FILLET THAT ENTERS THE BEGINNING OF THE RUMP. BUT TAKE IT WHOLE AND UNTRIMMED — IT'S MORE INTERESTING TO EAT, KEEPING ALL THE FAT ON IS IMPORTANT AND THAT BIT OF FILLET IS A BONUS.

SERVES 1–2

lamb rump	1, weighing 400-600g
Lamb Rub *(see page 118)*	30g
Maldon sea salt	
freshly ground black pepper	

Prepare a barbecue for smoking (see The Set-Up on pages 114–15) and set the temperature to 110°C. Be careful about using too much smoke as this can overpower the lamb.

To prepare the lamb, remove the skin from the top of the rump being careful not to rip off the fat with it. Rub the lamb all over with the lamb rub, shaking off any excess, and put it, fat side up, inside your barbecue. Smoke for 30–45 minutes, or until the internal temperature reaches 50–52°C. Remove from the barbecue and leave to rest while you adjust your barbecue for direct grilling (see page 112).

Season the rump with salt and pepper and grill for 1 minute on each side, or until evenly charred. Leave to rest for 5–10 minutes before carving.

Serve with Crispy Capers (see below).

CRISPY CAPERS

capers, drained	handful
oil, for deep-frying	

Heat the oil to 180°C in a deep-fryer or large saucepan.

Toss the capers into the fryer, and deep-fry for 1 minute, or until puffed and crispy. Drain on kitchen paper and serve.

LAMB BREAST

PERHAPS OUR FAVOURITE PART OF THE LAMB, THIS WAY OF COOKING LAMB BREAST
HAS BEEN ALMOST A CONSTANT ON THE MENU SINCE WE FIRST STARTED COOKING
IT. LAMB BREAST, ESSENTIALLY THE BELLY OF THE LAMB, IS FANTASTICALLY
FATTY, AND ROLLING THE BREAST MEANS THAT ALL THE FAT IS EVENLY SPACED
THROUGH THE FINAL ROLLED JOINT. A COOKED CROSS-SECTION OF THE BELLY IS
A BEAUTIFUL SIGHT, WITH LAYERS OF MEAT SANDWICHED IN BETWEEN FAT. THE
MERGUEZ SAUSAGE, OFTEN LEANER THAN A PORK SAUSAGE, WORKS WELL HERE, AS
THE RENDERING FAT FROM THE BELLY BASTES THE SAUSAGE MEAT DURING COOKING.
WE CHILL THE LAMB BREAST AFTER COOKING AND LET IT SET BEFORE SLICING
IT INTO THICK SLICES, THEN WE GRILL AND SERVE IT WITH CHEESE CURDS OR
SOURED CREAM AND LOTS OF CRISPY CAPERS.

SERVES 4

lamb breast	1, weighing about 1.3-1.5kg
Lamb rub (see page 118)	30g
merguez sausage	350g
Dijon mustard	20g
garlic cloves, minced	4

Prepare a barbecue for smoking (see The Set-Up on pages 114–15) and set the temperature to 110°C.

First, take your lamb breast off the bone. To do this, take the top layer of skin off the breast — it is thin but should be removed; take a sharp thin-bladed knife and find the seam between the skin and the fat that sits just beneath it. Pull the skin away from the fat being careful not to tear any of the fat or flesh on the breast.

To de-bone the breast, use the same knife and work your way along the breast, keeping as close to the rib bones as possible.

There should be no meat left on ribs once the breast has been removed. Once the breast bone has been removed, flatten the meat out, skin side down. Rub the exposed side of the breast evenly with the mustard and cover with half the lamb rub. Remove the sausage meat from the merguez sausage casing and spread it evenly over the mustard and rub, followed by the minced garlic.

Neatly roll up the lamb breast so only the skin side of the breast is exposed — think lamb Arctic roll! Tie the lambs breast, using butcher's string and make 4–5 evenly spaced knots.

Cover the rolled breast with the remaining rub and shake off any excess. Smoke in the barbecue for 6–7 hours, or until the internal temperature reaches 86–88°C and the lamb is soft to the touch.

At this point the breast can be carved with a very sharp knife, or chilled and then cut into slices and browned off in a hot pan. Serve with soured cream and pickles and Crispy Capers (see page 172).

MUTTON SHOULDER
& ANCHOVY HOLLANDAISE

> MUTTON SHOULDER IS A LITTLE TOUGHER THAN LAMB BUT HAS TWICE THE FLAVOUR, AND IF SLOW-COOKED OVER MANY HOURS, IT WILL DELIGHT.

SERVES 8

good Cantabrian anchovy fillets	10 g
capers	10 g
zest of 2 lemons	
zest of 1 orange	
apricot conserve	10 g
Dijon mustard	10 g
shoulder of mutton or lamb	1, weighing 2kg
Lamb Rub *(see page 118)*	75g
salt and pepper	
Pitt Cue Barbecue Sauce *(see page 122)*,	(optional)
Anchovy Hollandaise *(see below)*	100 g

Blitz the anchovies, capers, citrus zests, apricot conserve and mustard in a blender to a thick paste. Rub the paste all over the mutton shoulder and refrigerate overnight.

Prepare a barbecue for smoking (see The Set-Up on pages 114–15) and set the temperature to 110°C.

Take the mutton out of the fridge and cover it with the lamb rub. Put it in your barbecue and smoke for 10–11 hours, or until the internal temperature reaches roughly 87°C and the meat is very soft. Remove the meat from the barbecue and leave to rest, wrapped in foil, for 30 minutes. Pull the shoulder apart, season to taste (add barbecue sauce if necessary) and serve in Potato Rolls or London Bath Buns (see page 240), with lots of Anchovy Hollandaise and Burnt Leeks (see page 223).

ANCHOVY HOLLANDAISE

SERVES 8

good tinned anchovy fillets	150g
garlic cloves	3
thyme leaves	1 tsp
basil leaves	2
good mustard	1 tbsp
unsalted butter	250g
free-range egg yolks	4
white wine vinegar	100ml
shallots, peeled and sliced	3

Blitz the anchovies, garlic, thyme, basil and mustard in a blender to a smooth paste or on a board using a knife. Set aside.

Gently heat the butter in a small pan, then leave to stand. Skim off the solids on the top and pass the clarified butter through a fine sieve.

Place a heatproof bowl over a pan of gently simmering water. Add the egg yolks and vinegar and whisk together to form a hot foam, then turn off the heat. Slowly pour in the warm clarified butter in a steady stream, whisking constantly until all the butter is incorporated. Whisk the anchovy paste into the mixture and serve immediately.

HOT MUTTON RIBS

MUTTON BREAST OR BELLY IS ONE OF OUR FAVOURITE CUTS FROM THE SHEEP.
MUTTON IS LARGER THAN SPRING LAMB AND HAS A GREATER DEPTH OF FLAVOUR.

Prepare a barbecue for smoking (see
The Set-Up on pages 114–15) and set
the temperature to 110°C.

Carefully remove the top layer of skin
from the belly, then rub the mutton with
the lamb rub and shake off any excess.
Put it in your barbecue and smoke for 5–6
hours, or until the belly has a thick
bark but is gelatinous and soft, and the
internal temperature of the meat reaches
86°C. Remove from the barbecue and leave to
cool slightly. When cool enough to handle,
portion the belly into ribs.

Adjust the barbecue to direct grilling
(see page 112), then grill the ribs for
1 minute on each side until well browned.
Meanwhile, heat the hot sauce and barbecue
sauce together in a pan and keep warm.
When the ribs are cooked, toss them in
the sauce and serve at once.

A side of curd and Poor Man's Capers (see
page 193) would be welcome accompaniments.

SERVES 2

mutton belly (or lamb or hogget)	500g
Lamb Rub *(see page 118)*	50g
Hot Sauce *(see page 124)*	50ml
Pitt Cue Barbecue Sauce *(see page 122)*	50ml

WHOLE SPICY SMOKED
—— ROAST CHICKEN ——

WE BELIEVE IT'S ALMOST
IMPOSSIBLE TO IMPROVE ON A
SIMPLE ROAST CHICKEN, BUT THIS
IS JUST AS GOOD AND A BIT
DIFFERENT. THE MOST IMPORTANT
THING TO REMEMBER IS TO BUY
A GOOD BIRD — FREE-RANGE,
AND AS OLD AS YOU CAN FIND.
INTENSIVE FARMING PUTS BIRDS
ON THE SHELF AT SIX WEEKS OLD
(NOT GOOD), SO IF YOU CAN FIND
A BIRD THAT HAS LIVED FOR
A FEW MONTHS, YOU'LL BE
REWARDED.

SERVES 3–4

chipotle chilli paste	50g
unsalted butter	50g
maple syrup	50ml
roasted garlic paste	50g
House Rub (see page 119)	50g
free-range chicken	1, weighing 1.5kg

Blitz the chipotle chilli paste, butter, maple syrup, roasted garlic paste and house rub in a blender to a paste. Make slashes about 1cm deep in the thighs of the chicken with a sharp knife, then rub the chicken thoroughly inside and out with the paste, put it into a dish and leave overnight in the fridge.

Prepare a barbecue for smoking (see The Set-Up on pages 114–15) and set the temperature to 150°C.

Put the chicken, breast side up, into a roasting tray that will fit inside your barbecue and smoke/roast for 1½ hours, or until the internal temperature of the meat reaches 70°C and the juices run clear when the chicken is pricked with a knife at the thickest point of the thigh area.

Remove the chicken from the barbecue and leave to rest for 10 minutes before carving. Serve with Iceberg Salad (see page 210) and Anchovy Salad Cream (see page 205).

DEVILLED CHICKEN
— BUN —

AS BUNS GO THIS IS A REAL BEAUTY. IT STANDS VERY PROUD AND PRETTY ON
A PLATE, SERVED AS WE DO IN THE RESTAURANT WITHOUT THE LID IN PLACE
SO THE BRIGHT AND BEAUTIFUL PICKLED SALAD SITS ON FULL SHOW. THE EATING
OF IT HOWEVER, IS NOT SO PRETTY. THIS WAY OF FRYING CHICKEN WORKS REALLY
WELL, WITH THE PRESMOKING ALLOWING FOR A LIGHT CRUNCHY COATING THAT
KEEPS THIS BUN NICE AND CLEAN (ISH).

SERVES 2

free-range boneless chicken thighs	4
Master Chicken Brine (see page 90)	500ml
breakfast radishes, cleaned and leaves removed	20g
Smashed Cucumber and Pickled Watermelon Salad (see page 213)	80g
House Rub (see page 119)	30g
plain flour	100g
whole milk	100ml
oil, for deep-frying	
Chipotle and Maple Wings Marinade (see page 93)	50ml
London Bath Buns, sliced	2
Chipotle Mayonnaise (see page 198)	

Prepare a barbecue for smoking (see The Set-Up on pages 114–15) and set the temperature to 110°C.

Load the chicken thighs into the brine and refrigerate for 1 hour. Meanwhile, finely shave the radishes into a bowl of iced water. Once cold, drain the radishes and toss through the cucumber and watermelon salad.

Remove the thighs from the brine, dry on kitchen paper, then rub all over with the house rub and shake off any excess. Smoke the thighs in the barbecue for 1 hour, or until the internal temperature reaches 70°C. Remove from the smoker and leave to rest for 10 minutes.

Get ready two shallow bowls. In the first put the flour and in the second put the milk.

Coat the thighs in flour, shaking off any excess. Then dip the thighs into the milk, and then back into the flour. Heat the oil to 180°C in a deep-fryer or large saucepan, and deep-fry the thighs for 1-2 minutes, or until golden and crispy. Remove the thighs from the fryer, drain on kitchen paper and brush all over with the chipotle and maple marinade.

To construct the bun, toast the cut sides of the buns under a grill. Spread the chipotle mayonnaise on the base of the buns and top with the chicken thighs. Press the thighs down a little so the buns retain some structural integrity — these have a tendency to topple so a little force does it some good. Finish with the pickled salad on top and serve with the bun lids on the side.

WHOLE SMOKED
── DUCK ──

WE STARTED OFFERING WHOLE
DUCK FOR TWO OR THREE PEOPLE
TO SHARE, REMOVING THE CROWN
FOR SMOKING, DEEP-FRYING
THE WINGS AND MAKING SMOKED
CONFIT NUGGETS FROM THE LEGS.
AFTER THAT YOU ARE LEFT
WITH ALL THE LOVELY OFFAL
TO GRILL, SPREAD ON TOAST
AND PICK AT AS YOU WISH. IT
IS A GREAT WAY TO ENJOY A
DUCK, WITH LOTS OF DIFFERENT
FLAVOURS AND TEXTURES, BUT
UNFORTUNATELY IT IS TIME-
CONSUMING AND A LOT EASIER TO
DO IN A RESTAURANT KITCHEN
THAN AT HOME.

THIS METHOD OF SMOKING DUCK
IS INSPIRED BY THE TEA-
SMOKED DUCK OR ZHANGCHA
THAT IS A STAPLE OF BANQUETS
AND FEASTING IN THE CHINESE
PROVINCE OF SICHUAN. IT IS A
BRILLIANT WAY TO TREAT A DUCK
BUT REQUIRES A LITTLE BIT
OF ATTENTION. IN SICHUANESE
COOKING, THE DUCK IS
MARINATED, BLANCHED AND AIR-
DRIED BEFORE BEING SMOKED,
STEAMED AND DEEP-FRIED. EVEN
THE GREATEST DUCK FANATIC
IS GOING TO BE PUSHED TO DO
THIS ON A REGULAR BASIS, SO
THIS RECIPE IS SLIGHTLY MORE
SUBDUED, MAKING A MIGHTY FINE
FEAST ALL THE SAME.

SERVES 4

fresh Aylesbury duck	1, weighing about 2.5kg
Duck Rub *(see page 118)*	100g

TEA BRINE

water	1.5 litres
tea leaves (Oolong, Darjeeling or Lapsang Souchong)	50g
fresh ginger, peeled	2.5cm piece
bulb of garlic	1
star anise	2
soy sauce	100ml
honey	60ml
smoked Maldon sea salt	50g

In a large pan, whisk together all the brine
ingredients over a low heat until well
combined and the salt has dissolved. Chill
in the refrigerator.

Place the duck in a large bowl and pour over
the brine. Set aside and leave overnight.
Next day, remove the duck from the brine and
leave to dry in the fridge for an hour.

Prepare a barbecue for smoking (see The Set-Up
on pages 114–15) and set the temperature
to 170°C.

Rub the duck thoroughly inside and out
with the duck rub and shake off any excess.
Place it in the barbecue and smoke for
45 minutes—1 hour.

Remove the duck from the barbecue and leave
to rest for 10 minutes. Carve or pull the
duck apart, and serve hot with Potato Rolls
(see page 240), soured cream and pickles.

PULLED DUCK & CAVIAR BUNS

RICHARD CAME ACROSS THIS COMBO WHILE STAYING IN A POSH HOTEL IN ST PETERSBURG, RUSSIA. THERE, IT WAS ROAST DUCK AND CAVIAR, SERVED IN PANCAKES WITH A SHOT OF ICE-COLD VODKA. OUR VERSION SHOULD, OF COURSE, BE EATEN WITH A PICKLEBACK OR BOILERMAKER.

WE USE ETHICALLY FARMED CAVIAR, WHICH IS PRODUCED BY MILKING THE FISH OF THEIR EGGS RATHER THAN GUTTING THEM … LIKE A FISH.

SERVES 4

cucumber	1
leftover Smoked Duck *(see page 178)*	120g
Mother Sauce *(see page 120)*	40ml
Potato Rolls or London Bath Buns *(see page 240)*	4
soured cream	40ml
sturgeon caviar (Ossetra)	25g

Shave the cucumber lengthways into very thin strips. Place in iced water and set aside.

Pick the duck off the bone and heat through in a small pan with the mother sauce.

Drain the cucumber. Slice the buns in half and arrange a few strips of cucumber on the bottom half. Top this with the hot pulled duck, and finish with soured cream and caviar. Put the lid on and eat at once.

— DUCK GIBLET SAUSAGES —

IT'S NOT POSSIBLE TO GET MUCH
MORE DUCK INTO A SAUSAGE THAN
THIS, AND FOR THAT WE SHOULD
ALL BE VERY HAPPY.

IF PICKLED CHERRIES ARE NOT
IN YOUR STORE CUPBOARD, GET
PICKLING. AND IF YOU ARE NOT
YET PICKLING, SUBSTITUTE THE
CHERRIES WITH SOME PRUNES.
IDEALLY, CONFIT DUCK MEAT SHOULD
REMAIN IN THE FRIDGE FOR SEVERAL
WEEKS TO ALLOW THE FLAVOURS
TO DEVELOP, BUT WHO KNOWS
WHERE WE WILL BE IN SEVERAL
WEEKS, SO CRACK ON!

SERVES 6

duck necks, with skin	6
duck gizzards	12
duck wings	6
Duck Rub (see page 118)	10g
duck fat	250ml
duck hearts	12
duck livers	12
Pickled Cherries (see page 197), pitted	12
sprigs of thyme, leaves picked	2
Maldon sea salt	

Prepare a barbecue for smoking (see The Set-Up on pages 114–15) and set the temperature to 110°C.

Carefully remove the skin from the duck necks and try to keep the skin in one piece so that you can stuff them later. Season the gizzards, wings and skinned duck necks with some of the duck rub and place in a small cocotte dish. Cover with the duck fat, then place in the barbecue and smoke gently for 3 hours.

Season the duck hearts with more duck rub, add to the dish and cook for another 2 hours, then season the duck livers and add to the dish for a further 20 minutes. Remove everything from the barbecue and allow to cool slightly.

Take the duck necks and wings out of the dish, and leave any duck fat in the bottom of the dish. Pick all the meat from the bones and place in a bowl, then chop the other giblets and roughly chop the pickled cherries and thyme. Add to the bowl, season with salt and mix together, then refrigerate until needed.

Tie one end of each duck neck skin with string and stuff with the giblet mixture, then tie the other end. Place the sausages in the cocotte dish with the reserved duck fat and smoke for a further 30 minutes at 100°C. If you are not cooking these immediately, then drain on kitchen paper, and chill until you are ready to cook them.

Prepare a barbecue for direct grilling (see page 112). Remove the sausages from the dish, dry on kitchen paper and grill them until crisp and golden. Serve hot with salads and Pickled Pomegranate (see page 197) or chutney.

SMOKED QUAIL

WE STARTED SERVING QUAIL WHEN WE FIRST OPENED THE TRAILER, BUT A SINGLE SERVING OF ONE OR TWO BIRDS WAS NEVER REALLY ENOUGH. IT IS MUCH MORE SATISFYING TO HAVE A BIG PILE OF QUAIL IN FRONT OF YOU, KNOWING WHAT NEEDS TO BE DONE. QUAIL HAS SINCE BEEN DRESSED UP IN MANY WAYS ON OUR MENU, BUT THIS RECIPE IS SUPER SIMPLE AND TAKES ITS LEAD FROM THE LEGENDARY MENU AT ST JOHN WHERE WE HAVE ENJOYED MANY A QUAIL. ONCE YOU HAVE MASTERED SMOKING QUAIL DOWN TO A FINE ART, THEN IT IS DEFINITELY WORTH SUBSTITUTING ANY OF THE SMOKED WING SAUCES (SEE PAGES 92–3) FOR OUR MOTHER SAUCE.

SERVES 4

large oven-ready quail	8
Our Pickle Brine *(see page 78)*	2 litres
House Rub *(see page 119)*	100g
Mother Sauce *(see page 120)*	200ml

Load the quail into the brine and refrigerate for 2 hours. Remove from the brine and leave to dry.

Prepare a barbecue for smoking (see The Set-Up on pages 114–15) and set the temperature to 110°C.

Rub the quail inside and out with the house rub and shake off any excess. Place them on the barbecue and smoke for 30–40 minutes, or until the internal temperature reaches 64°C.

Remove the quail from the heat and adjust the barbecue for direct grilling (see page 112). Grill the quail for 30 seconds on each side, basting occasionally with the mother sauce, until well browned.

Remove from the grill and pile the quail into a serving bowl. Eat immediately.

CHAPTER

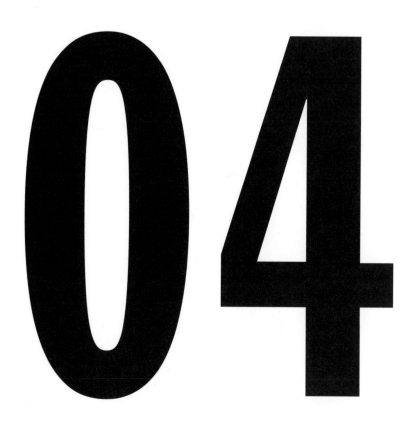

SLAWS
{&}
SIDES

SLAWS {&} SIDES

· · · · · · · · · · · · ·

Side dishes can really be anything you want them to be, and for this reason they are one of the most exciting things to cook and be faced with in a restaurant. Unfortunately, though, when it comes to barbecue, they are often neglected. Barbecue, as culture and technique, is based upon meat and the cooking of it over fire, so the neglect of side dishes is not entirely surprising. However, this neglect is a grave shame; for us, barbecue most definitely requires some satisfying respite and clean juxtapositions to the main meaty event. Side dishes are there to provide this balance.

The side dishes we have eaten on our trips to Texas, the neighbouring southern states and the barbecue in NYC have largely been disappointing, consisting mostly of sweet baked beans and overcooked greens. The vast majority of people eating barbecue, and travelling the vast distances that they do to eat at the most respected places, are not doing so for great side dishes, or even for any side dishes at all. We are guilty of the same thing when visiting Texas, largely in search of great smoked beef, but it was only through doing this that we began to realize the need for side dishes that offset and match the great meats on offer.

Perhaps our desire to focus a lot of time on side dishes and pickles comes from the fact that we have been brought up in restaurants where vegetables and fruits are given as much attention as the meat they sit alongside.

As a devout green hater, Simon would probably disagree, but whenever eating barbecue in the US, however awesome the meal may have been, we often exited the building on the brink of giving birth to a food baby – and this was down to the lack of balance in the meal. Delicious as it is, a tray of meat with no vegetables and just a small cup of meaty beans is not balanced and leads to some textbook post-meal lethargy shortly afterwards. That is not to say that our customers do not get into this state after eating with us, but we at least try to give them the option of a more civilized or balanced meal if they so wish.

The Soho kitchen has a small induction hob and no service oven, so the side dishes on our menu are dictated by what cooking equipment we can use during service and what can be used during the day. The one piece of equipment that is often available is the grill, so grilled vegetables was an obvious avenue for us to go down. Lettuces, onions, greens and brassicas have become some of our favourite vegetables to grill, developing sweet, complex, smoky flavours, and open up a huge number of options when it comes to delicious and simple side dishes. Next time you are making a salad or side dish, think seriously about using the grill. For us, the parameters of what can be a side dish are fairly loose. As long as you are using something seasonal and it helps to complete the meal, not becoming a meal unto itself, you are on the right track.

· · · · · · · · · · · · ·

PICKLES

PICKLING, FOR US, IS AN ESSENTIAL PART OF WHAT WE DO. SMOKED MEATS NEED SOME ASSISTANCE — A BIG MOUND OF MEAT IS A VERY ATTRACTIVE PROPOSITION, BUT WITHOUT GOOD SIDES AND PICKLES, KEY FOILS AND JUXTAPOSITIONS, THE MOUND BECOMES A MOUNTAIN.

PICKLING HAS ALWAYS BEEN AN OCCUPATION DICTATED BY THE SEASONS. THESE RECIPES CAN BE MADE BY ANYONE THROUGHOUT THE YEAR WITH WHATEVER FRESH VEG OR FRUIT IS AVAILABLE, BUT THEY WILL ALSO WORK TO FULFIL ANY IMMEDIATE DESIRE. IF YOU FIND YOURSELF IN NEED OF A PICKLE, YOU CAN EASILY KNOCK UP A PICKLE BEFORE LUNCH, AT ANY TIME OF YEAR. ON THE OTHER HAND, IF THERE IS A HUGE AMOUNT OF FRESH DAMSONS OR SLOES IN THE MARKET IN AUTUMN, YOU CAN GET PICKLING FOR THE WINTER.

THE PICKLE BRINE WE USE (SEE PAGE 78) IS A SIMPLE PICKLING BRINE AND IS IDEAL FOR A QUICK PICKLE THAT WILL LAST A WEEK, SOMETIMES A MONTH; HOWEVER, IT IS NOT A FULLY-FLEDGED FERMENTATION, SO BEST NOT TO LEAVE IT IN YOUR CUPBOARD FOR NEXT YEAR.

BREAD & BUTTER PICKLES

THESE ARE INTEGRAL TO THE RESTAURANT AND HAVE BEEN SERVED SINCE DAY ONE. THEY'RE SUPER EASY TO MAKE AND THEY STORE VERY WELL. THERE ARE NO EXCUSES NOT TO HAVE THEM IN YOUR FRIDGE JUST IN CASE. THEY'RE PURE JOY TO MAKE AND TO EAT.

RESERVE ALL THE PICKLING JUICE FOR MAKING PICKLEBACKS (SEE PAGE 23).

MAKES 1 LITRE

large cucumbers	5
onion	1
salt	80g

BRINE

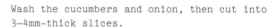

cider vinegar	300ml
soft brown sugar	200g
ground turmeric	5g
cloves	5
black mustard seeds	5g
fennel seeds	5g
coriander seeds	5g

Wash the cucumbers and onion, then cut into 3–4mm-thick slices.

Layer the cucumber and onion slices in a container, distributing the salt between the layers. Cover with clingfilm and put a heavy weight on top to help extract the water from the vegetables. Leave for at least 4 hours, until limp but crunchy.

When ready, pour away the liquid and rinse the cucumber and onion under running water, tossing constantly for 5–10 minutes, until no longer salty. Leave to dry.

Put the vinegar, sugar and spices into a stainless steel pan and stir over a medium heat until the sugar has dissolved. Bring to the boil, then add the cucumber and onion and cook for 3 minutes, or until the cucumbers have browned through but are not cooked. This is important, as overcooked cucumbers will soften. Remove from the heat and leave to cool.

Transfer the pickles to a sterilized jar (see page 78) and store in the fridge until needed, preferably leaving them for 2–3 weeks for a fuller flavour.

POOR MAN'S CAPERS

MAKES 1 LITRE

water	450ml
Maldon sea salt	50g
green nasturtium seeds	500g
Our Pickle Brine (see page 78)	500ml

Pour the water into a bowl, add the salt and stir to dissolve. Pick the nasturtium seeds while still green and put them into the water, then leave for 24 hours.

Drain and rinse the seeds, then pack them into sterilized glass jars (see page 78). Pour the pickle brine into a pan and bring to the boil. Pour the hot brine into the jars to cover the seeds, then seal. Leave for 2 weeks to mature before using.

PICKLED DAMSONS & SLOES

MAKES 1 LITRE

damsons or sloes	500g
soft light brown sugar	220g
red wine	180ml
red wine vinegar	120ml
small stick of cinnamon	1
cloves	4
coriander seeds	½ tsp
black peppercorns	5
small bay leaf	1

First, discard all the leaves and stalks from the fruits. Wash them gently under running water, but don't let them sit in the water for any length of time. Leave them to dry, then prick each fruit individually with a needle — a couple of pricks each is ideal.

Put the remaining ingredients into a pan and bring to the boil, then continue to boil for 10 minutes. The mixture will thicken just slightly. Take the pan off the heat and add the fruit. The aim here is not to burst or split the fruits and create chutney, but to keep them whole. Return the pan to a low heat and very gently bring back to the boil. If the fruits begin to split, lower the heat. Remove the pan from the heat once the mixture has come to the boil.

Transfer the fruit and liquid to sterilized glass jars (see page 78). Cover the exposed surface at the top of each jar with a circle of waxed paper, then seal and leave to cool. Store in the fridge for at least 2 months before using.

PICKLED BEETS

MAKES 1 LITRE

mixed beetroots (candy, yellow or red)	500g
water	230ml
white wine vinegar (or red, for red beetroots)	280ml
sugar	180g
Maldon sea salt	10g
shavings of fresh horseradish	10g
star anise	1
black peppercorns	3
small bay leaf	1

Steam the beetroots over a pan of simmering water until a skewer slides easily through the centre — this will take about 45 minutes to 1 hour, depending on size. When they're ready, remove them from the steamer, place in a bowl and cover with clingfilm. Leave for 15–20 minutes, or until the beetroots are cool enough to be handled and you can remove the skin easily with your fingers. Cut the beetroots whichever way you wish — wedges, slices, cubes all work well. Bring all the remaining ingredients to the boil in a large pan, then set aside and allow to cool.

Put the beetroots into a 1 litre sterilized jar (see page 78) or plastic containers and pour over the pickling liquid. The candy and yellow beetroots will discolour if they are used alongside red beetroots, so use separate containers for different colours.

Remove the horseradish shavings and bay leaf after a day, and leave the beets for a further 2–3 days before using. Keep refrigerated for up to 2 weeks.

· Alternatively, for a fresh instant pickle, pour cold Pickle Brine (see page 78) over shaved candy beetroot and add a pinch of ascorbic acid to hold the colour and serve. This makes for super good salads.

PICKLED CELERY

MAKES 1 LITRE

whole head of celery	1
Our Pickle Brine (see page 78)	500ml
black peppercorns	5
coriander seeds	1 tsp

Separate the celery into sticks. Cut roughly 5mm off the top and the entire white section off the bottom, roughly 2cm. Peel each stick to remove the outer fibres. This is important, as the pickled celery will be unpleasant if it contains lots of stringy bits. Slice the celery lengthways into 1cm-thick batons.

Put the pickle brine into a large pan and add the peppercorns and coriander seeds. Bring to the boil, then remove from the heat and add the celery. Leave to cool, then transfer to a 1 litre sterilized jar (see page 78) and refrigerate for 2–3 days before serving.

PICKLED CARROTS

MAKES 750ML

large carrots	5
Maldon sea salt	30g
caster sugar	180g
water	200ml
rice wine vinegar	200ml
star anise	1
fennel seeds, toasted	10g
coriander seeds, toasted	5g
black peppercorns	5g

Chop the carrots into batons or slices. Put them into a container and sprinkle with the salt and 20g of the sugar.

Move the carrots around so that they are evenly coated, then leave for 10 minutes, until the carrots are bendy. Wash them thoroughly and leave to dry.

Bring the rest of the ingredients to the boil in a stainless steel pan and drop in the carrots. Remove from the heat, leave to cool, then transfer to a sterilized 750ml jar (see page 78) or plastic containers and refrigerate for 3—4 days before eating.

· As an alternative, try adding the zest of ½ an orange, 2 cardamom pods, 1 cinnamon stick and 2 bay leaves to the brine.

PICKLED WATERMELON RIND

THIS IS A BRILLIANT PICKLE TO
MAKE FOR YOUR STORECUPBOARD
WHEN WATERMELONS COME
INTO SEASON. IT IS POPULAR
THROUGHOUT THE SOUTHERN US
STATES, BUT WE FIRST TRIED IT
AT FATTY CRAB IN NEW YORK'S
MEATPACKING DISTRICT. THEY
SERVED IT WITH PORK BELLY,
CHILLI AND CORIANDER. PORK
BELLY AND PICKLED WATERMELON,
AS IT TURNS OUT, IS AWESOME.

MAKES 600ML

rind of ½ a medium watermelon, including 1cm of red flesh	
good cider vinegar	230ml
water	130ml
caster sugar	100g
Maldon sea salt	10g
star anise	1
fresh ginger, peeled	1 small piece
stick of lemongrass, crushed	½

Cut the watermelon rind into 2.5cm-thick
slices. Carefully slice the skin off and cut
the slices into 2.5cm chunks.

Put the remaining ingredients into a large
pan and bring to the boil. Add the watermelon
rind and continue to boil for 1 minute.
Carefully transfer everything to a container,
then cool and refrigerate.

The pickles are ready in a few hours and
will keep for at least 2 weeks.

PICKLED POMEGRANATE

PICKLED CHERRIES

THIS IS A MIGHTY FINE PICKLE.
WE SERVE IT WITH SMOKED QUAIL,
GRILLED DUCK HEARTS AND SMOKED
LIVER AT THE RESTAURANT.
THE PICKLED SEEDS LOOK LIKE
JEWELS AND CAN TRANSFORM
A LIVER PÂTÉ OR ANY SALAD
INTO A THING OF BEAUTY. TRY
SHOOTING THE RESERVED PICKLE
JUICE AFTER A BOURBON FOR AN
INTERESTING PICKLEBACK.

THE CHERRY FARMS OF KENT ARE
AMAZING PLACES TO VISIT WHEN
FRUITING IS IN FULL SWING. YOU
WILL ARRIVE INNOCENT AND LEAVE
LOOKING LIKE A SLIGHTLY SICK
VAMPIRE. THE CHERRY IS ONE OF
OUR FAVOURITE BRITISH FRUITS,
AND IT'S ANOTHER ONE THAT
PICKLES VERY WELL.

MAKES 4 x 500ML JARS

large ripe pomegranates	4
good red wine	400ml
red wine vinegar	400ml
demerara sugar	400g
cloves	5
pink peppercorns	5
cardamom pods	3
star anise	1
stick of cinnamon	1
coriander seeds, toasted	1 tbsp
pared zest of ½ a large orange	

Cut the pomegranates in half and remove
all the seeds by tapping the back of the
pomegranate halves with a spoon. Put the
seeds into a bowl and discard any pith.

Put the remaining ingredients into a
large pan and bring to the boil, then set
aside to cool and infuse overnight. Pass
the liquid through a sieve, then add the
pomegranate seeds. Transfer to sterilized
jars (see page 78) and refrigerate for
2–3 days before using.

MAKES 2 x 400ML JARS

cherries	600g
white wine vinegar	500ml
water	250ml
light muscovado sugar	200g
stick of cinnamon	1
bay leaf	1

Rinse, dry and prick the cherries, then put
them into a plastic container.

Put the remaining ingredients into a large
pan and bring to the boil. Simmer for
5 minutes, then pour over the fruits and
leave for 3 minutes.

Pour into sterilized jars (see page 78),
cool, then put in the fridge to chill.
Allow to pickle for at least 2 weeks
before opening.

SLAWS

SLAW IS ONE OF THE MOST VERSATILE SALADS YOU CAN FIND. STARTING WITH
A SIMPLE BASE OF CABBAGE AND ONION YOU CAN DO PRETTY MUCH ANYTHING
YOU WANT AND BE INSPIRED BY FOOD FROM ALL OVER THE WORLD, ADAPTING
AND ADDING TO THE BASIC INGREDIENTS TO MAKE YOUR PERFECT SLAW.

CHIPOTLE & CONFIT GARLIC SLAW

SERVES 4–6

white cabbage, finely shredded	½
red cabbage, finely shredded	¼
sweetcorn kernels	200g
finely grated zest of 1 lime	
juice of 2 limes	
coriander, leaves picked	1 bunch
Chipotle Mayonnaise *(see right)*	150g
confit garlic cloves, puréed	6
Maldon sea salt	
freshly ground black pepper	
soured cream, to serve	
Pork Rub *(see page 118)*, to serve	

Put the shredded cabbages into a large bowl
and add the sweetcorn, lime zest, lime juice
and coriander and gently mix together.

Whisk together the chipotle mayonnaise and
garlic purée, add to the slaw and mix well.
Season with salt and pepper to taste.
To finish, top the slaw with a dollop of soured
cream and a generous shake of pork rub
before serving.

CHIPOTLE MAYONNAISE

MAKES 150G

mayonnaise	150g
chipotles in adobo, puréed	25g

Put the mayonnaise and puréed chipotles into
a bowl and whisk together. Store in the
fridge until needed.

RED SLAW

SERVES 6–8

large red cabbage, shredded	1
large red onion, finely sliced	1
large red pepper, deseeded and thinly sliced	1
large beetroot, peeled and cut into julienne strips	1
Pitt Cue Barbecue Sauce *(see page 122)*	250ml
Hot Sauce *(see page 124)*	100ml
salt and freshly ground black pepper	
soured cream, to serve	

Put the cabbage, onion, red pepper and beetroot into a large bowl.

Mix together the barbecue sauce and hot sauce and pour over the vegetables. Combine thoroughly, season to taste and refrigerate until chilled. Serve topped with soured cream.

KIMCHI SLAW

SERVES 4–6

smoked garlic clove	1
mayonnaise	100ml
lemon juice, to taste	
Chinese leaf cabbage, finely shredded	1
red onion, finely shredded	1
carrot, julienned	1
radishes, shaved and quartered	small bunch
Kimchi Hot Sauce *(see page 124)*	100ml

Make a smoked garlic mayonnaise by processing the garlic with the mayo in a blender and adding lemon juice to taste. Combine the cabbage, red onion, carrot and radishes in a bowl. Add the kimchi hot sauce and the smoked garlic mayo, mix gently together, then serve.

MUSTARD SLAW

SERVES 6–8

large white cabbage, shredded	¾
large white onion, finely sliced	1
large carrots, peeled and cut into julienne strips	2
sticks of celery, chopped	2
dill, chopped	bunch
hot mustard (English or Dijon for preference)	50g
cider vinegar	50ml
caster sugar	50g
mayonnaise	50ml
soured cream	50ml
salt	
freshly ground pepper	

Put the cabbage, onion, carrots, celery and dill into a large bowl.

In a separate bowl, mix together the mustard, vinegar, sugar, mayonnaise and soured cream and season to taste. Pour the dressing over the vegetables, adjust the seasoning and refrigerate until chilled.

GREEN SLAW

SERVES 6–8

large Savoy cabbage, shredded	1
onions, finely sliced	2
large green pepper, deseeded and finely sliced	1
large Granny Smith apple, skin on, cored and julienned	1
large jalapeño chilli, deseeded and finely sliced	1
coriander, chopped	½ small bunch
mint, chopped	½ small bunch
plain yogurt	100ml
finely grated zest and juice of 2 limes	
salt and sugar, to taste	

Put the cabbage, onions, green pepper, apple, jalapeño and herbs into a large bowl.

Mix together the yogurt, lime juice and zest, and add salt and sugar to taste. Pour over the vegetables, adjust the seasoning and refrigerate until chilled.

GREEN CHILLI SLAW

SERVES 6–8

white cabbage, finely sliced	½
red cabbage, finely sliced	¼
small bulb of fennel, finely sliced	1
mayonnaise	125g
coriander leaves	small handful
Maldon sea salt	

GREEN CHILLI DRESSING

green chillies	25g
fresh ginger, peeled and roughly chopped	25g
garlic cloves	25g
soft light brown sugar	25g
zest and juice of 1 lime	
coriander stalks, chopped	small handful
soy sauce	25g

To make the dressing, grill the chillies over direct heat on the barbecue or in a griddle pan until charred and blistered. Discard the stalks. Blitz all the remaining dressing ingredients except the soy sauce in a blender, adding the soy gradually until emulsified and smooth.

Lightly salt the cabbage and let it sit for 1 hour in a colander to allow the excess moisture to drain off. Transfer to a serving bowl and mix in the fennel. Add the mayo, coriander leaves and 50ml of the green chilli dressing and toss, then season with salt to taste. Add more dressing if you like, then serve.

VINEGAR SLAW

SERVES 6–8

fennel seeds	10g
small white cabbage	¾
small red cabbage	½
bulb of fennel	200g
red onions	2
mint tips	10
mixture of parsley, coriander and chervil	handful
Maldon sea salt	
freshly ground black pepper	

DRESSING

cider vinegar	100ml
white wine vinegar	100ml
extra virgin olive oil	70ml
caster sugar	70g
juice of 2 lemons	

Put the dressing ingredients into a bowl and whisk together until the sugar has dissolved. Set aside.

Toast the fennel seeds in a small pan until golden. Set aside.

Slice the cabbages, fennel and onions 1mm thick on a mandoline — the thinner the better — and put them into a large bowl. Finely chop the mint with a very sharp knife, pick the herb leaves and add to the bowl with the fennel seeds, making sure the herbs are spread evenly throughout the slaw.

Half an hour before serving, whisk the dressing again and pour over the slaw. Toss thoroughly and check for seasoning.

DRESSINGS

SALAD DRESSING

WE HAVE SIMPLE FRESH SEASONAL
SALADS ON THE RESTAURANT MENU
ALL YEAR ROUND, AND WE ALMOST
ALWAYS DRESS THEM SIMPLY —
GREAT OIL, LOTS OF LEMON
JUICE AND A FEW DROPS OF GOOD
VINEGAR. THIS DRESSING CAN BE
MADE IN ADVANCE, LEFT ALONE
AND JUST GIVEN A FINAL WHISK
BEFORE YOU DRESS YOUR SALAD.
BETTER-QUALITY INGREDIENTS
WILL IMPROVE IT GREATLY.
POOR OIL AND VINEGAR WILL NOT
MAKE FOR A GOOD DRESSING.

MAKES 150ML

extra virgin olive oil	100ml
juice of 1 lemon	
sherry vinegar	20ml
light brown sugar	10g
garlic clove, crushed	1
Maldon sea salt	
freshly ground black pepper	

Put all the ingredients into a bowl and
whisk together until fully emulsified.
Add salt and pepper to taste. Just before
you dress your salad, give the dressing
another whisk.

MEAD SALAD DRESSING

WE WENT THROUGH A BIT OF
A MEAD OBSESSION WHEN TOM
FOUND AN OLD BOTTLE AT HOME
AND A WINERY NEARBY THAT WAS
PRODUCING SOME FANTASTIC MEAD.
THIS SIMPLE SALAD DRESSING
WAS ONE OF THE MANY MEADY
THINGS BORN OUT OF THIS
SLIGHTLY UNUSUAL CRAZE AND
HELPS ADD COMPLEXITY TO
CLEAN, FRESH SALADS.

MAKES 150ML

extra virgin olive oil	100ml
cider vinegar	20ml
juice of 1 lemon	
medium-sweet mead	15ml
Maldon sea salt	
freshly ground black pepper	

Put all the ingredients into a bowl and
whisk together until fully emulsified,
seasoning to taste.

APPLE DRESSING

THIS IS A SIMPLE DRESSING,
BUT DELIGHTFUL. A VERY GOOD
APPLE JUICE IS ESSENTIAL, AND
NOT TOO SWEET. AS APPLE JUICES
AND VINEGARS ARE SO VARIABLE,
THIS RECIPE IS MORE OF A
GUIDELINE — TASTE AND ADJUST
UNTIL IT SUITS.

MAKES 250ML

extra virgin olive oil	100ml
unfiltered apple juice	120ml
cider vinegar	20ml
juice of 1 lemon	
Maldon sea salt	
freshly ground black pepper	

Put all the ingredients into a bowl and
whisk together until fully emulsified.
Add salt and pepper to taste.

This dressing can be stored in a sterilized
bottle (see page 78) in the fridge but will
need a good whisk before use.

ANCHOVY SALAD CREAM

HEINZ ALWAYS HELD THE SALAD
CREAM CROWN FOR US. NO ONE
COULD BEAT THAT INDUSTRIALLY
MADE, NUTRITIONALLY DUBIOUS
BOTTLE OF FILTHY GOODNESS.
THIS RECIPE GIVES IT A GOOD
GO AND CONTINUES ON THE
ANCHOVY THEME.

MAKES 700ML

cider vinegar	100ml
Dijon mustard	50g
caster sugar	10g
Maldon sea salt	10g
ground white pepper	¼ tsp
Cantabrian anchovy fillets	150g
garlic cloves	3
thyme leaves	1 tsp
double cream	400ml

Put all the ingredients except the cream
into a blender and blitz for 30 seconds.
Slowly add the cream, blitzing until
just incorporated.

Pass through a fine sieve and refrigerate
until needed.

APPLE, FENNEL, WATERCRESS — & RADISH SALAD —

APPLE AND FENNEL IS A SIMPLE BUT GREAT BASE FOR A SIDE SALAD
TO ACCOMPANY SMOKED PORK. BY ADDING PEPPERY RADISHES AND A
MEAD SALAD DRESSING, THIS HAS BECOME ONE OF OUR MOST POPULAR
SIDE SALADS IN THE RESTAURANT.

SERVES 3–4

bulbs of fennel, tops removed, fronds reserved	2
watercress	50g
Cox or Braeburn apples, cored	2
radishes, quartered	50g
mint leaves, torn	6
parsley leaves	10
chervil leaves	1 tbsp
Mead Salad Dressing *(see page 204)*	
salt, to taste	

Fill a small bowl with ice and water.

Wash the fennel, watercress, apples and radishes. Shave the fennel into the iced water, using a mandoline. Slice the apples into 2mm slices, then cut into batons. Drop the apples into the iced water, along with the radishes for 10 seconds.

Drain the apple, fennel and radishes and put them into a serving bowl with the fennel fronds. Add the herbs and watercress and toss together. Season with salt and dress lightly with the salad dressing. Serve immediately.

NASTURTIUM & TOMATO
— SALAD —

SERVES 3–4

bulbs of fennel	2
apples, cored	2
nasturtium leaves	60g
sweet cherry tomatoes, halved	10
Poor Man's Capers (see page 193)	20g
Mead Salad Dressing (see page 204)	
Maldon sea salt	
freshly ground black pepper	

THIS SALAD OWES ITS PLACE TO SEAN, THE MOST AMAZING VEG GROWER AND ALL-ROUND LEGEND, WHOSE FARM IS IN CORNWALL. ONE DAY, OUT OF THE BLUE, A PACKAGE ARRIVED AT PITT CUE ADDRESSED TO 'MAJOR TOM' CONTAINING LOTS OF SWEET LITTLE TOMATOES AND PEPPERY NASTURTIUMS. THESE ARE PARTICULARLY GOOD SERVED WITH SMOKED MEAT.

Shave the fennel into a bowl of iced water, using a mandoline. Cut the apple into 2mm slices, then cut into batons and add to the iced water. Drain the fennel and the apple. If the nasturtium leaves have thick stalks, slice these finely.

To assemble the salad, put the fennel, apple, nasturtium stalks and leaves, tomato halves and poor man's capers into a serving bowl and toss with the salad dressing. Season with salt and pepper and serve.

BIBB LETTUCE & HERB SALAD

WE LOVE BIG FLAVOURS BUT HAVE REALIZED THE IMPORTANCE OF HAVING SOME GREAT 'FOILS' UP OUR SLEEVE, SIDE DISHES THAT BALANCE THE BIG FLAVOURS IN THE MEATS. A HERB SALAD MAKES A GREAT JUXTAPOSITION FOR ALL THE FLAVOURS ASSOCIATED WITH BARBECUED FOOD. SIMPLE AND FRESH CERTAINLY HAS ITS PLACE, AND GOOD-QUALITY HERBS ARE ESSENTIAL.

SERVES 3–4

Bibb lettuce	1
Salad Dressing (*see page 204*)	20ml
chopped spring onions	1 tbsp
chopped coriander	1 tbsp
chopped parsley	1 tbsp
chopped mint	1 tbsp
Maldon sea salt	
freshly ground black pepper	

Pick and wash the lettuce leaves, then gently dry.

Just before serving, toss the leaves in the dressing with the chopped spring onions and herbs. Season to taste and serve.

ICEBERG SALAD

SERVES 4

iceberg lettuce	1
spring onions	1 bunch
onions	200g
pulled bread (bread torn into rough chunks)	80g
olive oil, for frying	
Pulled Pork Shoulder (see page 135)	100g
blue cheese	100g
buttermilk	100ml

Cut the iceberg lettuce into quarters and trim them into four small brick shapes. Cut the spring onions into very fine rings and set aside. Slice the onions.

Toast the pulled bread to make croutons.

Heat a little oil in a pan over a low heat, add the onions and cook, stirring until they are a lovely brown caramel colour. Remove them from the heat and mix with the pulled pork.

Put the blue cheese and buttermilk into a small bowl and mix with a fork, leaving the cheese slightly chunky.

Place each iceberg brick on a plate and dress liberally with the buttermilk blue cheese dressing. Top with the onion and pulled pork mixture, scatter over the spring onions and crumble the pulled bread croutons on top. Serve with a knife and fork.

PICKLED CARROT SALAD

LIGHTLY PICKLED VEGETABLES WORK REALLY WELL IN SALADS, BRINGING FRESHNESS AND AROMATIC NOTES FROM THE PICKLING BRINE. THIS CAME ABOUT BY ACCIDENT WHEN MAKING ANOTHER SALAD THAT WAS CLEARLY FAR LESS MEMORABLE!

SERVES 4

medium carrots, peeled and shaved	5
Our Pickle Brine (see page 78)	500ml
star anise	1
coriander seeds, toasted	10g
fennel seeds, toasted	10g
mint leaves, torn	10
coriander, finely chopped	small bunch
Maldon sea salt	

DRESSING

large garlic cloves, peeled and puréed	2
fresh ginger, peeled and puréed	thumb-sized piece
cider vinegar	45ml
caster sugar	10g
sesame oil	1 tsp
Maldon sea salt	

Put the carrot shavings into a container. Put the pickle brine into a pan with the star anise, coriander seeds and fennel seeds and bring to the boil. Pour the boiling pickle over the carrot and leave to cool, then refrigerate for 3 hours.

To make the dressing, combine the garlic, ginger, vinegar, sugar and sesame oil in a bowl and season with salt.

To assemble, put the carrot into a bowl, shaking off the excess pickle juice. Toss with the herbs, then season to taste and dress lightly. Toss again and serve.

SMASHED CUCUMBER & PICKLED WATERMELON SALAD

SERVES 6

cucumbers, peeled	4
watermelon flesh	200g
Pickled Watermelon Rind *(see page 196)*	200g
Pickled Carrots *(see page 195)*	100g
spring onions, sliced	5
green chillies, finely sliced	3
chopped coriander	3 tsp
chopped mint	5 tsp
salt	
freshly ground black pepper	

DRESSING

large garlic cloves, peeled and puréed	2
ginger, peeled and puréed	thumb-sized piece
cider vinegar	45ml
caster sugar	10g
sesame oil	1 tbsp
Maldon sea salt	

To make the dressing, combine the garlic, ginger, vinegar, sugar and sesame oil in a bowl and season with sea salt.

Peel the cucumbers, cut them into 6cm chunks, then crush them with the flat blade of a large knife. Chop the watermelon flesh into 3cm chunks and put them into a serving bowl with the cucumbers, pickled watermelon rind, pickled carrots and spring onions.

Just before serving, add the chillies, coriander and mint, season and toss with enough of the dressing to coat the salad.

THIS IS A GREAT LITTLE REFRESHMENT AMIDST THE MEAT FRENZY AT PITT CUE. IT WORKS REALLY WELL IN A PULLED PORK SANDWICH, BRINGING TO IT A HINT OF A VIETNAMESE BANH MI, WHICH THEMSELVES ARE ONE OF THE BEST PORKY DELIGHTS TO BE HAD. IN FACT, A HUGE AMOUNT OF ASIAN SALADS GO REALLY WELL WITH PULLED PORK AND BARBECUE FLAVOURS.

KIMCHI

KIMCHI HAD NOT FEATURED AT PITT CUE UNTIL RICHARD BREWED UP A BATCH FOR US ON THE TRAILER AND WE BEGAN TO REALIZE HOW MAGICAL THE COMBINATION OF BARBECUED MEAT AND KIMCHI CAN BE. IT CUTS THROUGH THE RICHNESS, AND ADDS LAYERS AND LAYERS OF FLAVOUR, TEXTURE AND HEAT AT THE SAME TIME. IT HAS MAGICAL BALANCING POWERS FOR EVEN THE FATTIEST OF PORK, SO IT'S NO SURPRISE THAT OUR PIG'S HEAD BUN HAS A HEALTHY AMOUNT OF KIMCHI IN IT.

IT'S IMPORTANT TO FIND THE RIGHT JARRED SALTED SHRIMP AND KOREAN CHILLI POWDER. WE MADE THE MISTAKE OF SUBBING IN SHRIMP PASTE FOR ONE BATCH. GREY FISHY KIMCHI IS NOT WHAT YOU WANT. ON WHICH NOTE, USE THE BEST ANCHOVIES YOU CAN FIND.

SERVES 8–10

small to medium Chinese leaf cabbage	1
Maldon sea salt	10g
caster sugar	75g
garlic cloves, minced	10
fresh ginger, peeled and minced	10 slices
Korean chilli powder	50g
tinned anchovy fillets	50g
light soy sauce	50ml
jarred salted shrimp	50g
spring onions, cut into 2cm batons	100g
carrots, cut into julienne strips	100g

Discard the outer leaves of the Chinese leaf cabbage. Cut it lengthways in half, then cut the halves crossways into 2.5cm-wide pieces. Put into a bowl and toss with the salt and 2 tablespoons of the sugar. Put into the refrigerator and leave overnight.

Put the garlic, ginger, chilli powder, anchovies, soy sauce, shrimp and remaining sugar into a large bowl and mix together. If the mixture is very thick, add water a little at a time until the mixture is just thicker than a creamy salad dressing but no longer a sludge. Stir in the spring onions and carrots.

Wash, drain and dry the Chinese leaf cabbage and add to the bowl. Cover and refrigerate. Though the kimchi will be tasty after 24 hours, it will be better in a week and at its prime in 2 weeks. It will still be good for another couple of weeks after that, though it will grow stronger and funkier.

MEAD BRAISED LETTUCE
—— CARROTS & ONIONS ——

MEAD IS HONEY WINE, AND IS ONE OF THE EARLIEST FORMS OF ALCOHOL TO BE RECORDED IN HISTORY. IT IS MADE BY FERMENTING A SOLUTION OF HONEY AND WATER, WITH SPICES, HOPS AND FRUITS OCCASIONALLY BEING USED AS FLAVOURINGS. IT IS PROBABLY BEST KNOWN FOR BEING THE TIPPLE OF CHOICE FOR FRIAR TUCK, ROBIN HOOD AND THE MERRY MEN OF SHERWOOD FOREST, BUT IS HAVING A WELCOME RESURGENCE NOW.

THIS RECIPE CAME ABOUT OVER A SUCKLING PIG AND COCKEREL DINNER IN PITT, WHEN WE FOUND A DUSTY OLD BOTTLE OF MEAD AND GAVE IT A GO. FOR GOOD REASON, EVERYONE KEPT GOING BACK FOR THE BRAISED VEG.

SERVES 6–8

large shallots	4
small carrots	200g
olive or rapeseed oil	25ml
garlic cloves	3
sprigs of thyme	3
smoked bacon lardons	100g
chicken wings	150g
chicken necks	3
Little Gem lettuces	8
cider vinegar	25ml
medium-sweet mead	150ml
chicken stock	200ml
Maldon sea salt	
freshly ground black pepper	

Peel the shallots and carrots and cut into quarters. Toss them with the oil, garlic and thyme, season with black pepper and a good teaspoon of sea salt and place them in a large casserole. Cook over a low heat on the hob, stirring occasionally, for 45 minutes, or until the shallots are darkly caramelized and sweet and the carrots are almost cooked through. Set aside.

In another pan, fry the bacon lardons, chicken wings and chicken necks until golden and crispy. Add the halved little gems and lightly fry in the bacon fat until golden. Transfer everything to the casserole, then add the vinegar and the mead.

Heat the oven to 180°C/350°F/gas mark 4.

Allow the vinegar and mead to reduce by a third, then pour in the chicken stock and cook in the oven for 30 minutes. Season to taste and serve.

GRILLED COURGETTES & TUNWORTH

WHEN COURGETTES ARE AT THEIR PRIME IN SUMMER, THEY ARRIVE IN THE KITCHEN BY THE BOX LOAD. SIMPLY DRESSING LIGHTLY WITH OIL AND SALT BEFORE GRILLING IS ONE OF THE BEST WAYS TO ENJOY THEM. HOWEVER, THIS HAS NOW BEEN TRUMPED BY THE INCLUSION OF TUNWORTH, A BRILLIANT ENGLISH CAMEMBERT-STYLE CHEESE THAT BECOMES SOFT AND GOOEY WHEN RIPE. OBVIOUSLY IT IS NOT TOO FOND OF A GRATER, SO ROLLING THE CHEESE INTO A SAUSAGE SHAPE AND FREEZING GETS ROUND THIS PROBLEM NICELY.

SERVES 6

ripe Tunworth cheese	1
courgettes	1kg
parsley leaves, finely chopped	10
thyme leaves	½ tsp
olive oil	15ml
juice of ½ a lemon	
Maldon sea salt	
freshly ground black pepper	

First, remove your Tunworth cheese from its packaging and wrapper. Spread out several large layers of clingfilm, then put the cheese on top and squeeze it into a rough sausage. If the cheese is very ripe you may have some leakage. Roll the Tunworth up in the clingfilm into a tight sausage and freeze.

When you are ready to cook, prepare a barbecue for medium-hot direct grilling. Alternatively, heat a griddle pan on the hob.

Cut the courgettes into 1cm slices — sharp diagonal slices always look best — and lightly oil them. Put them on the grill or griddle and cook for 5 minutes, until they are well charred but not cooked entirely through. Toss them in a bowl with the parsley, thyme, olive oil and lemon juice, and season to taste.

To serve, remove the Tunworth from the freezer and, while the courgettes are piping hot, grate over as much of the cheese as you wish. More the merrier.

SPROUT TOPS

SERVES 6

smoked bacon	50g
Brussels sprout tops	800g
smoked ham stock	300ml
cloves of garlic, peeled	3
Maldon sea salt	
freshly ground black pepper	

ANCHOVY BUTTER

Cantabrian anchovy fillets	125g
unsalted butter, softened and diced	250g
cayenne pepper	pinch
ground nutmeg	pinch
freshly ground black pepper	pinch
ground cinnamon	pinch
lemon juice	25ml
Worcestershire sauce	25ml
water	25ml

First make the anchovy butter. Put all the ingredients into a blender and blitz to a very smooth paste. Place the mixture on a few sheets of clingfilm and roll into a sausage about 3cm thick. Chill in the fridge (this will keep for up to 1 week).

Cut the bacon into small lardons and fry in a pan until crisp and golden. Drain on kitchen paper and reserve any fat from the bacon. It is not really needed for this recipe, but having bacon fat in the fridge is a bonus.

Remove the leaves of the sprout tops, discarding any very tough or damaged outer leaves, and cut the larger leaves into 2cm ribbons. The core of the sprout tops can be cut in half. Wash thoroughly to remove any dirt and grit. Blanch the cut leaves in boiling salted water for 10 seconds, then remove and plunge them into a container of iced water to cool. Once cold, drain thoroughly.

Put the ham stock into a pan and bring to the boil. Grate in the garlic and cook for 5 minutes. Reduce to a very gentle simmer and add the blanched sprout tops. Cook over a low heat for 15–20 minutes, until the leaves are softening but have not lost their freshness and colour. At the very last minute, season to taste with salt and pepper — although be warned that the bacon and anchovy will do much of the seasoning for you — and serve with 50g cubed anchovy butter and the lardons on top.

PURPLE SPROUTING BROCCOLI
WITH ANCHOVY & CHILLI

SERVES 4

butter	60g
red chillies, very finely sliced lengthways	2
Tabasco sauce	
purple sprouting broccoli	400g
parsley, finely chopped	small bunch
anchovy fillets	8
juice of 1 lemon	
Maldon sea salt	
freshly ground black pepper	

ANCHOVY IS A TRULY MAGICAL INGREDIENT THAT GOES WITH ALMOST ANYTHING. IT IS FANTASTIC WITH GRILLED MEATS, AND AS SUCH, WE CAN'T RESIST USING A LOT OF IT IN OUR SIDE DISHES. HOWEVER, IT'S VERY IMPORTANT TO BUY THE BEST YOU CAN AFFORD. A BAD ANCHOVY SHOULD NOT BE LET OUT OF ITS TIN.

Prepare a barbecue for medium-hot direct grilling (see page 112). Alternatively, heat a griddle pan on the hob.

In a small pan, melt the butter and add the chillies and 5 drops of Tabasco. Keep warm.

Wash the broccoli, and trim the stalks if necessary. Bring a pan of well-salted water to the boil and fill a container with cold water and ice. Add the broccoli to the boiling water and cook for 2 minutes, or until just starting to soften but still firm. Drain, then drop it into the iced water. Remove as soon as it is cold and drain on kitchen paper.

Grill the broccoli for 2 minutes, until just charred. The florets will char quickly, so keep moving the broccoli so that it grills evenly. Remove from the heat and put the broccoli into a serving bowl with the parsley, melted butter and chillies, anchovy fillets and lemon juice. Toss together and season to taste with salt and pepper (you may not need any salt, since the anchovies are already salty). Serve immediately.

BURNT HISPI CABBAGE
— WITH WILD GARLIC —

HISPI IS BEST FROM FEBRUARY TO
MAY AND COINCIDES NICELY WITH
THE WILD GARLIC SEASON, WHICH
STARTS IN THE WEST COUNTRY
FROM LATE FEBRUARY ONWARDS.

SERVES 2

green Hispi cabbage, quartered with outer leaves removed,	1
wild garlic	80g
extra virgin olive oil	
juice of ½ a lemon	
Maldon sea salt	
freshly ground black pepper	

Prepare a barbecue for medium-hot direct
grilling. Alternatively, heat a griddle pan
on the hob.

Bring a pan of salted water to the boil and fill
a container with cold water and ice. Add the
cabbage to the boiling water and cook for
1 minute, or until the core has softened only
slightly — you want it just undercooked.
Drain, then drop the cabbage into the iced
water, removing it as soon as it is cold.

Grill the cabbage for 1½ minutes on each side,
or until evenly charred. While it's still
hot, put it into a serving bowl and add the
wild garlic, a good glug of olive oil and
salt and pepper. Toss the cabbage with the
garlic leaves straight away so that
the garlic wilts with the residual heat.
Squeeze over the lemon juice and serve.

BURNT LEEKS
— WITH ANCHOVY HOLLANDAISE —

WE SERVE THIS AS A SIDE DISH
AT THE RESTAURANT, BUT IT WILL
ALSO MAKE A VERY FINE STARTER
OR SNACK, CONTINUING OUR
AFFAIR WITH OUR FISHY FRIEND.

SERVES 2

leeks, the younger the better	4
olive oil, for brushing	
basil, finely chopped, plus extra to serve	small handful
juice of 1 lemon	
Anchovy Hollandaise (see page 174)	100ml
Maldon sea salt	
freshly ground black pepper	

Prepare a barbecue for medium-hot direct grilling. Alternatively, heat a griddle pan on the hob.

Wash the leeks and peel off the outer layer. Trim away 1cm at the root end and leave just a few centimetres of green at the top end.

Bring a pan of well-salted water to the boil, and fill a container with cold water and ice. Add the leeks to the boiling water and cook for 5 minutes, or until softened. Drain, then drop them into the iced water. Remove when cold and drain on kitchen paper. Brush the leeks with olive oil and grill for 2–3 minutes, turning occasionally, until charred. Put them into a bowl with the basil and lemon juice and toss together, then season to taste. Spoon the anchovy hollandaise over the top, sprinkle with basil and serve.

— BURNT CORN ON THE COB —

THIS WAS, IN FACT, ONE OF THE FIRST EVER SIDES SERVED AT THE PITT CUE TRAILER. A FRIEND OF OURS SHOWED US A NEAT TRICK OF COOKING THE COBS WITH THE HUSKS ON, THEN PEELING THEM BACK AND TWISTING THEM AROUND THE VERY BASE OF THE COB TO MAKE A TEMPORARY HANDLE. THE HUSKY HANDLE WORKS MUCH BETTER THAN THOSE USELESS MINI FORK THINGS THAT ARE ALWAYS SOLD IN JULY WHEN CORN IS PROLIFIC.

SERVES 1

corn on the cob, husk still intact	1
unsalted butter	20g
House Rub *(see page 119)*	10g

Prepare a barbecue for medium-hot direct grilling. Grill the corn, husk on, for 20 minutes, until almost all the layers of husk and fibre have burnt through and the kernels are nearly exposed.

Remove from the grill and peel back the remaining pieces of husk. Brush the corn with the butter and sprinkle with the house rub before serving.

— GRILLED BABY GEMS —

THE BABY GEM DEVELOPS A REAL MEATINESS ONCE COOKED, WHICH IS OBVIOUSLY SOMETHING THAT APPEALS TO US.

SERVES 6

Baby Gem lettuces	6
olive or rapeseed oil	20ml
Maldon sea salt	
freshly ground black pepper	

Prepare a barbecue for medium-hot direct grilling.

Cut the baby gems in half. Rub the cut sides with some of the oil and season with salt and pepper. Place the baby gems, cut side down, on the hot grill and close the lid. Cook for 5 minutes, untouched.

Open the barbecue and check the baby gems. Their faces will be slightly blackened. Turn them over and cook for a further 2 minutes, then remove from the grill, dress with the remaining oil, season to taste and serve.

— MASH —

MASH HAS NEVER REALLY LEFT THE
MENU AT PITT CUE, ALBEIT APPEARING
IN DIFFERENT GUISES. IT IS MADE
FRESH FOR EVERY SERVICE, ALWAYS BY
HAND, AND THE POTATOES ARE ALWAYS
BAKED. THE BENEFITS OF BAKING THE
POTATOES ARE TWOFOLD: FIRSTLY, THE
POTATOES DRY OUT BETTER, MAKING FOR
A SMOOTHER MASH AND GIVING A SMOKY
BAKED NOTE TO THE MASH; SECONDLY,
YOU WILL HAVE LOTS OF EMPTY POTATO
SKINS TO FILL WITH WHATEVER
DELIGHTS YOU FANCY. LONG LIVE
BAKED MASH.

SERVES 6—8

baking potatoes, Maris Piper if possible	2.5kg
double cream	275ml
chilled unsalted butter, diced	175g
Maldon sea salt	

Heat the oven to 200°C/400°F/gas mark 6.

Wash the potatoes and let them dry, then bake
them in the oven for roughly 45 minutes to
1 hour, or until cooked through. When they
are ready, gently heat the cream in a large
pan. Remove the potatoes from the oven, cut
them in half, then leave them for 1 minute
to allow some of the moisture to evaporate.

Scoop the potato flesh from the skins (reserve
the skins for loading, see opposite) and
pass it through a fine sieve into the cream,
pushing it through with the back of a
spatula or a pastry scraper. Work quickly,
as the potato needs to be sieved while still
hot. Start to beat the mix together with the
spatula while adding the diced butter, until
it is smooth and silky. Season to taste with
salt. Keep warm. Mash needs to be eaten
fresh and does not keep well.

· One of the many joys of a baked potato is the skin it leaves behind; the perfect potato 'spoon' to be filled with whatever you fancy. We deep-fry our leftover skins, give them a liberal shake of dry rub when they leave the fryer, then load then with all sorts. Brisket, picked beef ribs, ox cheek, pig's head, confit duck, duck offals and pulled pork have all been topped with bone marrow, kimchi, pickles, fruit ketchup, cheese sauce, piles of chopped herbs and anything else we can find. More a meal than a mouthful, but that is yet to cause complaint. Another excuse to make more mash potato then.

LARDO & ROSEMARY MASH

SERVES 6–8

Mash *(see page 226)*	1kg
Mother Sauce *(see page 120)*	200ml
lardo di Colonnata, chilled	150g
small garlic clove, minced	1
sherry vinegar	5ml
sprig of rosemary, leaves finely chopped	1
freshly ground black pepper	

Heat the mash and mother sauce in two separate pans.

Mince the lardo through the smallest setting on a meat mincer and put it into a bowl. Add the garlic and vinegar and begin massaging air into the lardo with a spatula, as if you were making a good mash. As you work with the meat, folding in air, it will get softer. Beat continuously for 5 minutes, until the lardo is light and fluffy. Add the rosemary and pepper to taste.

Top each portion of hot mash with a teaspoon of whipped lardo, pour over the hot mother sauce and serve.

BURNT ENDS MASH

SERVES 6–8

Mash *(see page 226)*	1kg
Pitt Cue Burnt Ends *(see page 158)*	200g
Mother Sauce *(see page 120)*	200ml

Heat the mash, burnt ends and mother sauce in separate pans. Accompany each portion of mash with a good spoonful of the burnt ends and pour over the sauce. Serve immediately.

BONE MARROW MASH

SERVES 6–8

Mash *(see page 226)*	1kg
Mother Sauce *(see page 120)*	200ml
Whipped Bone Marrow *(see below)*	150g

Heat the mash and mother sauce in two separate pans. Get the marrow up to room temperature.

To serve, dot teaspoons of marrow over the mash and pour over the hot mother sauce. Watch the marrow melting slowly into the sauce before diving in!

WHIPPED BONE MARROW

split shafts of centre cut shin bone, marrow scooped out	4
juice of ½ a lemon	
garlic clove, minced	1
flat-leaf parsley, finely chopped	small handful
Maldon sea salt	
freshly ground black pepper	

Put the raw marrow, lemon juice and garlic into a blender and blitz for 10 minutes, until very smooth, glossy and nicely whipped. Everything should be fully combined. Pass through a sieve, then fold the parsley into the mixture and season to taste.

—— DUCK & HOMINY HASH ——

A HASH RUNS VERY CLOSE TO CROSSING THE LINE BETWEEN A SIDE DISH AND A FULL MEAL UNTO ITSELF. IN FACT, IT PROBABLY DOES CROSS THE LINE, AND THUS RENDERS ALL OUR TALK OF WHAT MAKES THE PERFECT SIDE DISH REDUNDANT. IT IS THE EGGS FAULT. REMOVE THE EGG AND IT IS A SIDE DISH, BUT THE EGG REALLY IS WHAT REALLY MAKES THIS HASH HAPPEN, LEAKING INTO THE SWEET SHALLOTS, DUCK AND CRISPY POTATOES. THIS HASH IS ALSO THE COMPLETE BREAKFAST, AND THEREFORE THE PERFECT ALL-ROUNDER!

HOMINY IS TREATED DRIED MAIZE KERNELS FROM WHICH THE HULL AND GERM HAVE BEEN REMOVED. NOT TOO COMMON IN THE UK, AND PERHAPS MOST OFTEN SEEN AS A SNACK, PUFFED UP AND ROASTED WITH SPICES AND SALT, IT IS A STAPLE IN MEXICAN CUISINE. IT IS A SIMPLE PULSE, A THRIFT INGREDIENT THAT IS ANOTHER FANTASTIC VEHICLE FOR OTHER THINGS. IT CAN BE FOUND IN WEST INDIAN AND MEXICAN STORES IN TINNED AND DRIED FORM. DRIED HOMINY NEEDS TO BE SOAKED AND COOKED. IF YOU CAN'T FIND IT, USE SWEETCORN INSTEAD.

SERVES 6

potatoes	250g
sweet potatoes	250g
reserved duck fat	70ml
banana shallots, diced	4
garlic cloves, minced	2
cooked or tinned hominy	250g
leftover Smoked Duck (see page 178)	250g
thyme leaves	½ tsp
free-range duck eggs	6
Maldon seas salt	
freshly ground black pepper	
chopped parsley, to finish	1 tbsp

Peel and chop the potatoes and sweet potatoes into 2cm dice. Steam the diced potato until just cooked.

Put 20ml of the duck fat into a pan with the shallots and garlic and cook until they are soft and beginning to caramelize. Set aside.

Heat another 30ml of duck fat in a large non-stick pan and add the cooked potatoes, hominy, smoked duck, thyme leaves and shallots and garlic. Cook for 25 minutes, tossing occasionally to evenly crisp and caramelize the hash.

Heat the remaining 20ml of duck fat in a hot non-stick pan and fry the duck eggs. The yolks should still be runny.

Season the hash with salt and pepper to taste and serve each helping with a fried egg and a good amount of parsley on top.

PUMPKIN HOME FRIES
WITH NDUJA MAYONNAISE

NDUJA IS A DEEP-RED, SPICY
CALABRIAN SALAMI MADE FROM
PORK FAT AND THE JOWLS OF
THE PIG, AND SOMETIMES THE
TRIPE. UNLIKE A FRENCH SEC
OR MOST ITALIAN SALAMIS IT
REMAINS SPREADABLE, THUS
LENDING ITSELF TO RUNNING
THROUGH SAUCES AND AS A
CANDIDATE FOR AN
AWESOME MAYONNAISE.

SERVES 6

lardo di Colonnata, cut into 5mm dice	50g
pumpkin flesh, cut into 1cm dice	500g
Maris Piper potatoes, cut into 1cm dice	500g
rosemary leaves, finely chopped	1 tsp
salt and pepper	

NDUJA MAYONNAISE

nduja	50g
Dijon mustard	15g
lemon juice	15ml
garlic clove, minced	1
free-range egg yolks	2
groundnut oil	200ml
olive oil	50ml
salt	

Bring all the mayonnaise ingredients to room
temperature. Put the nduja into a blender
with the mustard, lemon juice and garlic and
blitz to a purée. Set aside.

Whisk the egg yolks in a bowl, then add a
pinch of salt and continue to whisk until
thick, roughly 45 seconds. Slowly add the
groundnut oil, whisking continuously until
the mixture begins to thicken. When it has
thickened and the oil is all incorporated,
add the olive oil and whisk until thick
and glossy. Whisk in the nduja mixture and
season to taste. Refrigerate until needed.

Heat 50g of lardo in a large non-stick pan.
When it's hot and melted, add the pumpkin
and potatoes and cook over a high heat for
15 minutes, or until the vegetables are
crisp and cooked through. Remove from the
heat, toss in the chopped rosemary leaves
and season to taste. Serve immediately,
with a large blob of nduja mayonnaise.

—— HOG MAC 'N' CHEESE ——

A DOUBLE DOSE OF PORK —
CRISP BACON RUB BREADCRUMBS
ON TOP AND QUIVERING CHUNKS
OF BELLY WITHIN — ADDS
RICHNESS AND TEXTURE TO ELBOW
MACARONI. THE SAUCE IS A
MIX OF STILTON, CHEDDAR AND
OGLESHIELD CHEESES.

SERVES 6

dried elbow macaroni	500g
cooked bacon or pork belly (or any leftover smoked meat), cut into chunks	200g
breadcrumbs	100g
Smoked Bacon Rub (see page 119)	50g
Cheddar, grated	100g

CHEESE SAUCE

whole milk	600ml
butter	60g
shallots, minced	2
garlic cloves, minced	2
sprigs of thyme, leaves picked	2
plain flour	60g
Colston Bassett Stilton or Stichelton cheese, grated	125g
Montgomery Cheddar cheese, grated	125g
Ogleshield cheese, grated	125g
salt	1 tsp
ground white pepper	½ tsp

Bring a large pan of salted water to the boil and cook the pasta until al dente. Drain, then refresh in cold water and drain again. Put into a large bowl and add the cooked bacon or pork belly.

To make the cheese sauce, put the milk into a medium pan, bring to a foamy boil, then reduce the heat to low and keep warm.

In another pan, melt the butter over a medium heat. Add the shallots, garlic and thyme leaves and cook for 10 minutes, or until the onions and garlic are just caramelizing and soft.

Whisk in the flour and continue to cook until a pale 'roux' has formed. Then, whisking steadily, ladle the hot milk into the roux a cupful at a time, completely incorporating each amount before adding the next. After all the milk has been added, continue to whisk until the sauce thickens and bubbles gently (about 2 minutes).

Add the stilton, Cheddar, Ogleshield, salt and pepper and stir until completely melted.

Heat the oven to 180°C/350°F/gas mark 4.

Stir three-quarters of the cheese sauce into the cooked pasta and bacon. Layer the pasta in a large ovenproof gratin dish and spread the rest of the cheese sauce over the top. Lightly toast the breadcrumbs and mix with the bacon rub and Cheddar, then scatter evenly over the top cheese sauce layer.

Bake in the oven for 20 minutes, or until golden and bubbling. Serve with a side of Devilled Pigs' Feet for pouring over (see page 145). Any leftovers can be used in Trailer Trash (see page 138).

HOG 'N' HOMINY

THIS IS A DUBIOUSLY TERMED 'SIDE DISH'. WE ORIGINALLY MADE THIS FOR SHARING, WITH A WHOLE SMOKED PIG'S CHEEK SUNK INTO THE TOP OF THE HOMINY AND CHEESE MIXTURE AND DEVIL DIP GRAVY POURED OVER. ABSOLUTELY FILTHY: A PORK OVERLOAD. SO NUTRITIONALLY QUESTIONABLE WAS THIS AS AN ACCOMPANIMENT TO MEAT, IT WAS ARCHIVED IN FAVOUR OF SOMETHING A TOUCH MORE RESERVED, AN ACTUAL SIDE DISH UP TO THE TASK AND ONE THAT DOESN'T LEAVE YOU FULL FOR A DAY OR TWO. THIS MAKES A GREAT ALTERNATIVE TO MAC 'N' CHEESE.

SERVES 6

butter	50g
shallots, sliced	2
spring of thyme	5
garlic cloves, crushed	2
smoked bacon, diced	200g
Cheese Sauce (see page 235)	600g
soured cream	150ml
hominy, drained	2 x 475g cans
Maldon sea salt	
freshly ground black pepper	

Melt the butter in a large saucepan, add the shallots, thyme and garlic and cook over a gentle heat for 10 minutes, or until soft and beginning to caramelize.

In a separate non-stick pan, cook the bacon over a high heat for 5–10 minutes, or until golden and crispy.

Add the cooked bacon, cheese sauce, soured cream and hominy to the shallot mixture, season with salt and pepper and continue cooking over a gentle heat for 10 minutes.

Meanwhile, heat the oven to 180°C/350°F/gas mark 4.

Put the hominy mixture into a baking dish, then cook in the oven for 30 minutes, or until golden.

BAKED BEANS

EVERYONE LOVES A BAKED BEAN. FEW
OTHER THINGS CAN BE BREAKFAST,
SECOND BREAKFAST, BRUNCH, LUNCH,
AFTERNOON SNACK AND DINNER.
TINNED PRE-COOKED BEANS WORK WELL,
BUT THEY WILL NEVER BE AS GOOD
AS DRIED BEANS. THE LITTLE EXTRA
EFFORT IS WELL WORTH IT. SIMILARLY,
BUYING READY-MADE PASSATA WILL
WORK, BUT IT WILL NOT COMPARE.

THIS RECIPE CALLS FOR THE PASSATA
TO BE SMOKED, AS THAT'S WHAT WE
DO IN THE RESTAURANT. HOWEVER, AN
OVEN-BAKE ALSO WORKS VERY WELL.

SERVES 4–6

BEANS

dried mixed beans, soaked overnight	250g
Whipped Bone Marrow (see page 228)	50g
bacon, finely diced	50g
ham stock	100ml
leftover Smoked Brisket (see page 156)	80g
Pitt Cue Barbecue Sauce (see page 122)	80ml
Maldon sea salt	
freshly ground black pepper	

PASSATA

olive oil	10ml
large onion, diced	½
garlic cloves, minced	3
smoked paprika	1 tsp
cloves, crushed	5
tinned tomatoes	250g
cider vinegar	10ml
light brown sugar	10g

Drain the soaked beans, then cover them with
fresh water and boil until just tender.
Drain and set aside.

If using a barbecue, prepare it for smoking
(see The Set-Up on pages 114–15) and set the
temperature to 150°C.

To make the passata, heat the olive oil in
a flameproof pan that will fit inside your
barbecue and sweat the onion in the oil for
5 minutes, or until soft. Add the garlic,
paprika and cloves and cook for a further
5 minutes. Add the tomatoes, vinegar and
sugar, stir, then smoke in the barbecue
for 1 hour, or until the passata is smoky
and thickened.

Adjust the temperature of the barbecue to
170°C, or preheat your oven to 150°C/300°F/
gas mark 2.

Fry the bacon in a pan for 10 minutes, or
until golden and crispy. Put the bacon
into an ovenproof pan that will fit inside
your barbecue, along with any bacon fat
rendered during frying, and add all the
other ingredients as well the passata.
Mix the beans mixture thoroughly, then
smoke or oven-bake for 30 minutes, or until
a crust begins to form and most of the
liquid has been absorbed.

Remove the beans from the oven and stir.
The sauce should be thick. If the beans are
too dry, loosen the sauce with some more ham
stock or water. Season to taste. The beans
can be served immediately, but will improve
after 2 days in the fridge. We reheat them
with Mother Sauce (see page 120) and whisk
through more whipped bone marrow paste
before serving.

POTATO ROLLS

MAKES 12

dried yeast	10g
sugar	10g
warm water	100ml
free-range egg	1
warm milk	150ml
warm Mash *(see page 226)*	100g
strong white flour	500g
Maldon sea salt	10g
warm rendered bacon fat	100ml
butter	50g

GLAZE

milk	50ml
free-range egg yolks	2
Maldon sea salt	10g

Combine the yeast, sugar and water in a small bowl and set aside for 15 minutes.

Knead together the egg, milk, mash and yeast mixture on a slow speed. Add the flour and salt and knead for a further 5 minutes.

Add 75ml of the bacon fat, 15ml at a time, until the dough is smooth and homogenous. Transfer to an oiled bowl and leave in a warm place for about 40–60 minutes, until doubled in size.

On a lightly floured surface, punch the dough down, then knead it for a minute. Divide it into 12 equal pieces. Roll each piece into a ball in the palm of your hand and gently press it down. The dough will be very soft, so it may not form perfect rolls.

Melt the butter and pour it on to a baking tray along with the remaining 25ml of bacon fat. Place the dough balls, seam side down, on the baking tray 6cm apart from each other, and leave in a warm place for 45 minutes, or until doubled in size again.

Heat the oven to 190°C/375°F/gas mark 5. Gently whisk together the milk and egg yolks for the glaze. Bake the rolls in the oven for 15 minutes, then brush the tops of the rolls with the glaze and sprinkle over the salt. Put back into the oven and bake for a further 10–15 minutes, until lightly brown. Cool on a wire rack for 15 minutes before serving.

LONDON BATH BUNS

MAKES 12

milk	300ml
fresh yeast	15g
strong white flour	450g
granulated sugar	5g
Maldon sea salt	5g
butter	200g

Put the milk into a pan and warm to blood temperature. Crumble in the yeast.

In a separate bowl, mix the flour, sugar and salt. Add the butter and rub in with your fingertips.

Add the milk mixture and mix to form a dough, then cover the bowl and leave in a warm place for an hour or so to prove.

Grease a baking tray with butter and sprinkle it with flour. Divide the dough into pieces weighing about 70g each and place them on the baking tray. Leave in a warm place to prove for a further 30 minutes.

Meanwhile, heat the oven to 190°C/375°F/gas mark 5. Bake the buns for 20 minutes, then remove from the oven and set aside to cool.

JALAPEÑO & SOURED CREAM CORNBREAD

THIS IS A GREAT CORNBREAD RECIPE AND COMES FROM A FAMILY FRIEND IN CALIFORNIA (A FELLOW MIDDLE WHITE AND MANGALITZA BREEDER, FUNNILY ENOUGH). IT WORKS REALLY WELL WITH HOT WINGS, NOT LEAST BECAUSE CORNBREAD, HOT MEATY THINGS AND CURD ARE LOVELY TOGETHER.

SERVES 4–6

baking powder	2 tsp	vegetable oil	180ml
Maldon sea salt	1 tsp	free-range eggs, gently beaten	2
yellow cornmeal	220g	soured cream	230ml
hot chillies, e.g. jalapeño (pickled jalapeños work well), finely chopped	2	tinned creamed corn	460g
		onion, grated	1
		good Cheddar cheese, grated	100g

Heat the oven to 170°C/325°F/gas mark 3 and butter a 20 or 23cm ovenproof baking dish or cake tin.

Put the baking powder, salt, cornmeal and chillies into a medium bowl and mix together. In another bowl, mix together the oil, egg, soured cream and creamed corn. Mix the grated onion into the wet ingredients, then quickly mix this into the dry ingredients.

The batter will be a little lumpy and clumpy — this is a good thing. Pour half the batter into the pan and sprinkle 75g of the Cheddar on top. Pour in the remaining batter and top with the rest of the Cheddar.

Bake in the oven for 45 minutes, or until the surface feels firm and a skewer inserted comes out clean. Leave for 10 minutes to cool a little, then cut into wedges. This is best served hot, and don't refrigerate it or it will ruin the texture.

POPOVERS

THE POPOVER IS AN AMERICAN
VERSION OF YORKSHIRE PUDDING,
WHICH HAS BEEN MADE IN
ENGLAND SINCE THE SEVENTEENTH
CENTURY, THOUGH IT HAS
EVOLVED AND IS TYPICALLY
BAKED IN MUFFIN TINS. THE
NAME COMES FROM THE FACT THAT
THE BATTER SWELLS OR 'POPS'
OVER THE TOP OF THE TIN
WHILE BAKING.

MAKES 12

plain flour	200g
free-range eggs, beaten	200ml
fennel seeds, ground	pinch
freshly ground black pepper	pinch
semi-skimmed milk	200ml
beef dripping	

Put the flour, eggs, ground fennel seeds, black pepper and milk into a bowl and mix together. Put into the fridge and leave, covered, overnight.

Next day, heat the oven to 220°C/425°F/gas mark 7. Put a little dripping into 12 mini individual tins set on a baking tray or into each hole in a muffin tin, then put them into the oven until the dripping is smoking. Pour in the batter to come halfway up the tins or holes, and bake until the tops pop over like muffin tops. After another 15 minutes, remove the tray from the oven and turn out the popovers, then put them back into the oven directly on the oven shelf to crisp them underneath.

Serve with the Smoked Standing Rib Roast (see page 164).

SWEET
STUFF

SWEET STUFF

. . . .

We have a love affair with desserts: the creamy, the cakey, the sticky, the clean, the buttery, the set, the soft, the cold, the hot, the elegant and the slutty. Especially the slutty.

The kitchen in Soho has no identifiable pastry section. A small corner on top of a boxed-in boiler, a covered vegetable sink that doubles up as our bun-making area next to the dishwasher that hands out free steam facials every five minutes – this area constitutes the pastry section which has been the bane of everyone who has worked there. This, combined with a domestically retarded oven constantly full of baked potatoes that tries to sabotage any decent pastry work, meant the odds were against us when it came to offering a little post-meat sweetness.

In Soho we started by offering two desserts every day each service, and that is something we stick to, keeping them simple, with one often offering some clean, fruity respite and the other a bit of pudding sluttiness. Whether or not eating in a dark Soho basement affects the sensibilities, it would seem that the slutty desserts tend to outsell the more restrained ones. That said, a slightly camp posset seems to go down well.

. . . .

— BANOFFEE MESS —

SERVES 4

Meringues *(see below)*	2
Bourbon Caramel Sauce *(see page 276)*	200ml
bananas, sliced	2
Whipped Custard *(see page 254)*	200ml
Shortcakes *(see below)*	4
frozen chocolate bar (we use Snickers)	1

MERINGUES

free-range egg whites	125ml (about 4-5 eggs)
caster sugar	250g
chopped nuts of your choice, toasted and cooled	50g

SHORTCAKES

butter	350g
caster sugar	170g
plain flour	225g
toasted breadcrumbs	100g
ground almonds	170g
finely grated zest of 2 oranges	

First, make the meringues. Heat the oven to 140°C/275°F/gas mark 1. Using a free-standing mixer, whisk the egg whites until almost stiff, then slowly add half the sugar and continue mixing until the whites become stiff and glossy. Using a metal spoon, fold in the remaining sugar and whatever toasted nuts you are using.

Line a baking sheet with greaseproof paper, using a little of the meringue mixture underneath to prevent the paper moving about. Spoon neat individual meringue portions on to the greaseproof. Place in the oven and immediately reduce the temperature to 110°C/225°F/gas mark ¼. Bake for 45 minutes, then remove from the oven and leave to cool. These meringues store well in a sealed container for up to 2 days.

Next, make the shortcake. Using a free-standing mixer, cream the butter and sugar for 10 minutes, until fluffy and pale. Fold in the remaining ingredients and combine well. Take three sheets of greaseproof paper and divide the mixture equally between them. Roll the greaseproof and form into sausages about 7cm thick, then tie the ends. Chill in the fridge for 2–3 hours, until firm.

Meanwhile heat the oven to 150°C/300°F/gas mark 2 and line two baking sheets with greaseproof paper. Unwrap the dough, slice it into 6mm rounds and lay them on the baking sheets. Bake for 15 minutes, or until golden, then leave to cool. You will need 2 or 3 shortcakes, crumbled, for the mess.

In a large bowl, gently fold together 2 crushed meringues, a quarter of the bourbon caramel sauce, 8 slices of banana and the whipped custard.

To assemble the mess, make a 1cm layer of crumbled shortcake in the base of four small glass tumblers. Layer some of the banana slices on top, followed by a thin layer of bourbon caramel sauce. Top this with 2 tablespoons of the custard meringue mixture and then another layer of crumbled shortcake. Finish with a layer of whipped custard, more slices of banana and a drizzle of the remaining sauce. Take the chocolate bar straight from the freezer, grate generously over the top and serve.

THIS IS BEST EATEN AT
A TIME WHEN YOU WILL
NOT FEEL GUILTY ABOUT IT —
HANGOVERS, BREAK-UPS AND
ILLNESS CAN ALL BE
REMEDIED WITH A GOOD MESS.

DO NOT FORGET TO GRATE OVER
THE FROZEN CHOCOLATE BAR.

THIS IS NOT A PRODUCT PLUG — 'PEANUT, BOURBON,
MALT, CHOCOLATE AND CARAMEL MESS' IS JUST TOO SCARY
A PROSPECT TO EAT. WE ARE NOT AFTER A LIFETIME
SUPPLY OF SNICKERS — THE ENJOYMENT WOULD BE FAR
OUTWEIGHED BY DENTISTRY BILLS. THERE IS NO DENYING
A DEEP LOVE FOR THIS BAR, THOUGH. EATING ONE
STRAIGHT FROM THE FRIDGE, WHEN THE CHOCOLATE AND
CARAMEL NEED EXTRA WORK TO GET THROUGH, IS THE ONLY
WAY TO DO IT. THIS IS A SLUTTY SALUTE TO THE GREAT
BAR AND THAT FRIDGE-COLD ENJOYMENT.

'SNICKERS' MESS

SERVES 4

vanilla pod	1
double cream	90ml
malt powder (such as Ovaltine)	10g
Meringues *(see page 248)*	2
Brownies *(see below)*	50g
Bourbon Caramel Sauce *(see page 276)*	80ml
Peanut Butter Ice Cream *(see page 268)*	2 tbsp
frozen milk chocolate bar, or a Snickers	1

Split the vanilla pod and scrape out the seeds. Make a malt cream by whisking the double cream with the malt powder and vanilla seeds until it forms soft folds. Set aside.

To assemble the mess, break the meringues into bite-sized chunks and break the brownies into small pieces. Put them into a mixing bowl, add the malt cream and half the bourbon caramel sauce, and gently fold together.

To serve, spoon the meringue mixture into four serving bowls. Top with the ice cream, pour over the remaining sauce and finish by shaving over the frozen chocolate bar.

BROWNIES

MAKES 12–16

dark chocolate (70% cocoa solids)	300g
butter	350g
vanilla pod	1
large free-range eggs	5
caster sugar	300g
plain flour	160g
cocoa powder	50g
Maldon sea salt	4g

Preheat your oven to 180°C/350°F/ gas mark 4 and line a 20 x 30cm baking tin with baking parchment.

Melt the chocolate and butter in a heatproof bowl set over a pan of gently simmering water, making sure the base of the bowl doesn't touch the water. Remove and set aside.

Split the vanilla pod and scrape out the seeds. Whisk the eggs in a bowl with the sugar and vanilla seeds until thick enough to coat the back of a spoon. In a separate bowl, mix the flour, cocoa and salt together. Stir the melted chocolate mixture into the egg mixture, then fold in the flour mixture.

Pour the mixture into the baking tin and bake for about 20–25 minutes, until just set on top.

Remove from the oven and allow to cool, then put into the fridge and leave overnight to firm up.

FRUIT & WHIPPED
——— CUSTARD MESS ———

THIS RECIPE AND THE PROCESSES
INVOLVED REMAIN PRETTY MUCH
THE SAME FOR MOST FRUITS WHEN
THEY COME INTO SEASON.
WHILE WE ADD HOMEMADE
MARSHMALLOWS IN THE
RESTAURANT, THEY CAN BE TIME
CONSUMING TO MAKE AND ARE
DEFINITELY OPTIONAL FOR THOSE
WHO ARE PUSHED FOR TIME.

SERVES 3–4

fresh fruit, plus extra to decorate	
(see below)	500g
caster sugar	100g
juice of 2 lemons	
demerara sugar	50g
Peanut Meringues (see page 248)	2
Marshmallows (see page 254), (optional)	
Whipped Custard (see page 254)	100ml

First, purée the fruit. Put 300g of
fruit into a pan with the caster sugar
and the juice of 1 lemon and cook gently
over a low heat for 10 minutes, stirring
occasionally. Pass the mixture through
a fine sieve and set aside. (For damsons
and sloes, combine in a roasting tin
with three times the amount of sugar and
100ml water, and bake in the oven at
150°C/300°F/gas mark 2 for 15 minutes.)

Put the rest of the fruit into a container,
add the juice of the remaining lemon and
the demerara sugar and set aside for a few
hours to macerate.

To assemble the mess, put 2 crushed
meringues into a bowl and gently combine
with 2 tablespoons of fruit purée,
1 tablespoon of macerated fruit, a few
marshmallows (if using) and 3 tablespoons
of whipped custard. Spoon into a serving
bowl and top with the fruit, the remaining
macerating liquid, and a good helping
of marshmallows. If you like, light a
blowtorch and toast the marshmallows
until dark and molten.

· This mess undoubtedly works best with berry fruits.
Strawberries, raspberries, blueberries, redcurrants,
blackcurrants, blackberries, gooseberries; all create
a lovely mess. Stone fruits like sloes and damsons
also work well, and rhubarb is a fixture on the menu
throughout its forced season.

· Walnuts, almonds and pistachios all work well
instead of peanuts in the meringues.

· Substitute vanilla cream for the custard if you are
up against it.

MARSHMALLOWS

MAKES LOTS

gelatine leaves	12g (about 1-2)
water	30ml
caster sugar	200g
liquid glucose	20g
fresh free-range egg whites	80g (about 4 eggs)
finely grated zest of 1 lemon	
fruit purée, optional	80g
cornflour, for dusting	70g
icing sugar, for dusting	70g
Maldon sea salt	pinch

Line a baking tray with greaseproof paper. Put the gelatine leaves into a bowl, cover with cold water and leave to soak until soft. Put the 30ml water, caster sugar and glucose into a large pan and heat until the temperature reaches 121°C on a sugar thermometer.

In a free-standing electric mixer, slowly whisk the egg whites and lemon zest on a medium speed until they reach stiff peaks.

When the sugar mixture reaches temperature, take the pan off the heat. Squeeze out the gelatine leaves and add to the pan, mixing gently. Be careful: the mixture may bubble and splutter a bit. Turn the mixer to the lowest setting. With the mixer running, gently pour the hot sugar mixture down the side of the bowl into the egg whites, then increase the speed to medium and continue to mix until the whites are cool, glossy and stiff, about 8–10 minutes. Fold in the fruit purée, if using, until well combined.

Scoop the mixture into a piping bag with the smallest nozzle available. Combine the cornflour and icing sugar and sift over the prepared baking tray — this will stop the marshmallows from sticking. Pipe little marshmallow teardrops on to the greaseproof, about the width of a 10p piece with a nice quiff. Put the tray into the fridge for 1 hour to allow the marshmallows to set.

WHIPPED CUSTARD

MAKES 850ML

large free-range egg yolks	6
caster sugar	65g
vanilla pod	1
double cream	700ml

Whisk the egg yolks and sugar in a very large bowl until light and fluffy. When you lift the whisk, it should make thick ribbons in the mixture.

Split the vanilla pod and scrape out the seeds. Put 600ml of the cream into a large pan with the vanilla seeds and heat slowly until steaming, just below boiling point. Slowly whisk the hot cream into the egg yolk mixture until well combined.

Half fill a very large bowl or a sink with water and ice and let a smaller bowl chill in the water. Keep it upright, as the cream will need to be strained into this chilled bowl.

Return the mixture to the pan over a low to medium heat and slowly whisk continuously until thickened, about 5–7 minutes. If it begins to boil, remove from the heat and whisk to ensure it does not split. The custard should be very thick.

Pass the custard through a sieve into the chilled bowl and stir for a few minutes, to cool it down as quickly as possible. Cover the bowl with clingfilm and refrigerate until well set.

When you are ready to serve the custard, whisk in the rest of the cream until it forms thick peaks.

PIMM'S MESS

WHEN THE CLEVER CHAPS AT THE
ICE CREAM UNION DROPPED OFF
A TUB OF PIMM'S SORBET DURING
OUR FIRST SUMMER IN SOHO WE
THOUGHT THEY WERE JOKING.
WHAT EVIL GENIUS WOULD
PRODUCE A PIMM'S SORBET, NOT
ONE THAT TASTES OF THE LIQUOR
ITSELF, BUT OF THE FINISHED
CONCOCTION; THE STEEPED
CUCUMBER, STRAWBERRIES AND
TORN MINT THAT MAKE A WELL-
MADE PIMM'S SO GOOD? IT HAD
TO BECOME A DESSERT, AND SO
THIS CLEAN LITTLE MESS WAS
BORN. IT BEGAN WITH VERY
FINE SLICES OF APPLE, BUT
WAS MADE AGAIN AT THE END OF
THE SUMMER USING OUR CERAMIC
BARBECUE AND SOME SLOWLY
COOKED PEARS THAT TURN SUPER
SWEET AND A LITTLE SMOKY WHEN
COOKED THIS WAY.

SERVES 2

Comice or Conference pear	1
caster sugar	30g
strawberries	80g
balsamic vinegar	10ml
zest of ½ an orange	
juice of ½ a lemon	
mint leaves	10
Meringue (see page 248), broken up	1
Pimm's Sorbet (see page 280)	2 scoops

Prepare your barbecue for medium-heat direct grilling, about 150°C. Chop 5mm off the base of the pear so that it sits flat, with the flesh exposed on the bottom. Dip the exposed base into the caster sugar, then place the pear on buttered greaseproof paper on the grill and close the lid. Cook for 30 minutes, until the pear is soft and the skin has begun to shrivel. Remove from the heat and set aside.

Put half the strawberries into a pan and add the balsamic vinegar, orange zest, lemon juice and 10g of the caster sugar. Cook over a gentle heat until the strawberries are just softening, then remove from the heat and blitz in a blender until smooth. Pass through a sieve and set aside.

Finely chop 6 of the mint leaves, then use a pestle and mortar to grind thoroughly with the remaining caster sugar to make a mint sugar. Cut the rest of the strawberries in half, place in a bowl with the mint sugar and leave to macerate for 1 hour, tossing occasionally.

To serve, cut the pear into quarters and remove the seeds, peel and core. Slice the quarters in half. Arrange these slices in a shallow bowl and add the macerated strawberries and shards of meringue alongside. Top with a scoop of Pimm's sorbet and the rest of the mint leaves, torn roughly, then drizzle the strawberry coulis on top.

ORANGE & CHOCOLATE CHEESECAKES

SERVES 8

water	300ml
caster sugar	200g
large oranges	5
Grand Marnier	50ml
packet of chocolate biscuits (we use Oreos)	1
milk chocolate, to grate over	

CHEESECAKE TOPPING

vanilla pod	1
cream cheese (Philadelphia is best)	1.3kg
free-range eggs	6
free-range egg yolks	4
double cream	200ml
caster sugar	200g
finely grated zest of 1 lemon	
finely grated zest of 1 lime	
finely grated zest of 1 orange	

THIS IS NOT A CONVENTIONAL CHEESECAKE IN ANY SENSE, BUT RATHER MORE OF A CUSTARD MADE WITH CREAM CHEESE. THE RECIPE CAME ABOUT IN THE KITCHEN WHEN WE BEGAN MAKING OUR OWN CREAM CHEESE, BUT AS IT TURNS OUT IT'S PRETTY HARD TO BEAT PHILADELPHIA.

THE FINISHED MIX WILL BE THICKER THAN A CUSTARD BUT BY NO MEANS SET. WE PIPE THE MIX ON TO POACHED FRUITS AND JELLIES, AND ADD SHORTCAKES AND CRUMBS TO BUILD A 'CHEESECAKE'. ONCE YOU HAVE THIS RECIPE NAILED, THE OPTIONS FOR VARIATIONS ARE ENDLESS.

To make the cheesecake topping, split the vanilla pod lengthways and scrape out the seeds. Put them into a heatproof bowl with the rest of the cheesecake topping ingredients and set over a pan of gently simmering water for 20 minutes, whisking constantly until smooth and thickened. Pass through a fine sieve and chill in the refrigerator.

Pour the 300ml water into a large pan, add the sugar and heat gently to dissolve.

Peel and segment the oranges, removing any skin and pith, put the segments into a bowl and set aside. Squeeze any orange juice remaining in the debris into the pan with the sugar syrup. Add the Grand Marnier to the pan and bring to the boil, then remove from the heat and pour over the orange segments. Leave to cool slightly, then cover with clingfilm and set aside to cool completely.

To make each cheesecake, put 5 or 6 orange segments in the bottom of 8 small clean jars and add a little of the liquid. Crumble over a cookie and use a piping bag to pipe the cheesecake topping mixture over the top, to reach just below the surface of the jar.

Grate the chocolate evenly over the top and serve.

LEMON & CHERRY POSSETS
—— WITH FRUIT MARSHMALLOWS ——

A CUTE, CITRUSY AND VELVETY
POST-PORK REFRESHMENT.
THESE POSSETS CAN BE MADE
WELL IN ADVANCE AND WILL SUIT
ALL SORTS OF FRUIT, WHICH
MAKES IT A PRETTY PERFECT
GET-ME-OUT-OF-THE-SHIT
DESSERT CANDIDATE.

SERVES 5–6

cherries	500g
demerara sugar	40g
blackcurrant jam	20g
vanilla pod, split lengthways	1
double cream	600ml
caster sugar	170g
lemon juice	100ml (about 2 lemons)
Marshmallows *(see page 254)*	

Set aside a cherry for each posset, to use as a garnish. Remove the stones from the remaining cherries and cut them all in half. Put half the cherries into a bowl with 20g of the demerara sugar and set aside to macerate for 1 hour.

Put the rest of the cherries into a pan with the other 20g of demerara sugar, the blackcurrant jam and the split vanilla pod and cook on a low heat for 10 minutes, until softened. Remove the vanilla pod, blitz the cherries to a thick pulp in a blender and pass through a sieve to make a thick purée. There should be about 70–80g. Set aside.

Divide the macerated cherries evenly between serving glasses, reserving the juices. The cherries should just cover the bottom of the glass. Put the glasses into the refrigerator to chill.

To make the posset, bring the cream and sugar to the boil in a pan, whisking to ensure that the sugar is well combined. Take the pan off the heat and pour in the lemon juice, then pass the mixture through a fine sieve. Take the glasses out of the fridge and pour the posset on top of the cherries. Allow to cool, then return the glasses to the fridge for 4 hours to set.

To serve, arrange the marshmallows on top of each posset. If you like, you can blowtorch the marshmallows until just browned and melting. Finish with a cherry on top.

— OLD-FASHIONED JELLY —

ONE OF OUR FAVOURITE
COCKTAILS MADE INTO
A DESSERT. SERVE WITH A
BIG SCOOP OF ICE CREAM
FOR A NIGHT CAP AND
A DESSERT ALL IN ONE.
MAKE SURE YOU FIND THE
RIGHT CHERRIES, AS IT
MAKES A BIG DIFFERENCE
TO THE FINAL JELLY.

SERVES 4–5

gelatine leaves	4g
soda water	80ml
bitters syrup (see below)	80ml
maraschino cherry juice	30ml
bourbon	80ml
maraschino cherries, halved and pitted	5

BITTERS SYRUP

water	175ml
granulated sugar	100g
Angostura bitters	50ml

First, make the bitters syrup. Put the
water, sugar and bitters into a medium pan.
Place over a medium heat and allow the sugar
to dissolve completely, then bring to the
boil, stirring occasionally, and boil for
5 minutes. Remove from the heat and allow
to cool to room temperature.

To make the jelly, put the gelatine into
a bowl, cover with cold water and leave
to soak until soft. Combine the soda
water, bitters syrup and cherry juice in
a small pan. Squeeze out the gelatine, add
to the pan and heat over a very low heat for
about 5 minutes, stirring constantly, until
it has dissolved. Remove from the heat,
add the bourbon and stir until combined.

Pour the liquid into ramekins or a mould.
Evenly distribute the cherry halves
through the mixture and refrigerate until
fully set. Serve with Prune & Whiskey
Ice Cream (see page 268).

TOFFEE APPLE GRUNT

THIS PUDDING SHARES MANY OF THE SOOTHING QUALITIES THAT A COBBLER OR CRUMBLE HAS, BUT IS, FOR SOME REASON, MORE APPEALING. IT IS EQUALLY GOOD COLD, SO MAKE A LARGE GRUNT AND FINISH IT OFF FOR BREAKFAST. THIS RECIPE WAS WRITTEN ON A RAINY DAY AND FEELS LIKE IT SHOULD BE EATEN ON THAT SORT OF DAY WITH SOME SWEET MULLED CIDER OR JUST SOME DECENT BOURBON FOR COMPANY. IT IS LIKE A HOT TODDY AND PILLOW ALL ROLLED INTO A SMALL DESSERT POT.

SERVES 4

caster sugar	200g
Cox, Braeburn or Russet apples, peeled, cored and sliced into $\frac{1}{8}$ slices	800g
vanilla pods, split lengthways	2
cinnamon stick	1
star anise	1
finely grated zest of 1 lemon	
pine nuts, toasted	100g
bourbon-soaked agen prunes, roughly chopped	12
rum	40ml
blackberries	200g

ALMOND COOKIE TOPPING

free-range egg whites	2
ground almonds	180g
caster sugar	100g
almond essence	10ml

ALTERNATIVE BUTTERMILK BATTER TOPPING

plain flour	70g
ground almonds	60g
baking powder	1 tsp
bicarbonate of soda	¼ tsp
Maldon sea salt	1 tsp
cinnamon sugar	30g
unsalted butter, melted	60g
buttermilk	130ml

Put the sugar into a pan over a medium heat and cook without stirring until it turns into a thick, golden caramel. Add the apples, split vanilla pods, cinnamon, star anise and lemon zest to the pan. Cook for 10—15 minutes, stirring occasionally, until the apples just retain some shape and take on some colour and the mixture is thick. Add the prunes, pine nuts and rum, stir gently and cook for a further 5 minutes. Set aside to cool.

For the almond cookie topping:
Heat the oven to 170°C/340°F/gas mark 3½.

Beat the egg whites until stiff peaks form. Gently fold in the ground almonds and sugar, then add the almond essence and fold gently until well combined. Set aside.

Half fill four ramekins or a mini casseroles or cast-iron pot with the apple mixture. Sprinkle the fresh berries over the apple mixture and top with tablespoons of the almond batter topping. Bake in the oven for about 15 minutes, or until the batter topping is golden and slightly puffed up. Leave to cool for 10 minutes, then dust with icing sugar and eat with ice cream, fresh berries and cold custard.

For the buttermilk batter topping:
Heat the oven to 180°C/350°F/gas mark 4.

Sieve together the flour, ground almonds, baking powder, bicarbonate of soda, salt and sugar. Stir in the melted butter and add enough buttermilk to form a soft and fairly wet dough.

Half fill four mini casseroles or cast-iron pots with the apple mixture. Sprinkle the fresh berries over the apple and top with tablespoons of the batter. Bake for about 20 minutes, or until the dough has slightly puffed up and turned golden.

Leave to cool for 10 minutes, then dust with icing sugar and eat with ice cream, fresh berries, and some cold custard.

DOUGHNUTS

BROOKE SMITH, A SPOKESPERSON FOR
KRISPY KREME SAYS, 'DOUGHNUTS
ARE A NORMAL PART OF A HEALTHY,
BALANCED DIET.'

OUR ADVICE WOULD BE TO EAT UNTIL
JUST BEFORE THE POINT OF REGRET —
ABOUT THREE DOUGHNUTS, WE RECKON.

MAKES 25

warm milk	225ml
dried yeast	14g (2 sachets)
light muscovado sugar	20g
butter	225g
free-range eggs	5
Maldon sea salt	pinch
strong white flour	450g
oil, for deep-frying	
caster sugar and ground cinnamon, for rolling	

Place the warm milk, yeast and half the muscovado sugar in a bowl and mix well to combine. Cover with a damp tea towel and leave in a warm place for 15 minutes.

In a large bowl, beat the remaining muscovado sugar with the butter until creamy, then add the eggs one by one until each are incorporated. Add the yeast mixture, the flour and salt and beat until smooth. Put the damp tea towel on the top and refrigerate overnight.

When you're ready to cook the doughnuts, heat the oil to 170°C in a deep-fryer or large saucepan.

Turn out the dough on to a lightly floured surface and roll out until 3cm thick. Use a 5cm diameter biscuit cutter to cut out circles, then drop them straight into the oil. Deep-fry the doughnuts in batches, 3–4 at a time, for 2 minutes each side, or until golden. Place on kitchen paper to drain, then roll them in caster sugar and cinnamon while still hot.

Alternatively, use a piping bag with a fine plain nozzle to fill the doughnuts with Creamy Vanilla Filling or Chocolate Frosting (see page 266) and leave to set.

CREAMY VANILLA FILLING

MAKES ENOUGH TO FILL 25 DOUGHNUTS

vanilla pod	1
free-range egg yolks	6
maple syrup	100ml
double cream, chilled	1 litre
bourbon	100ml

Split the vanilla pod and scrape out the seeds. Put the egg yolks and maple syrup into a large bowl and whisk until light and fluffy. When you lift the whisk, it should make thick ribbons in the mixture.

Pour half the cream into a bowl and put into the fridge to use later. Pour the other half into a large pan and add the vanilla seeds and bourbon. Heat slowly until steaming, just below boiling point. Slowly whisk the hot cream into the egg mixture until well combined.

Half fill a very large bowl or sink with water and ice and let a smaller bowl chill in the water. Keep it upright, as the custard will be strained into this chilled bowl.

Return the cream and egg mixture to the pan and set over a low—medium heat, and slowly whisk until thickened, about 5—7 minutes. Do not let it boil — if it does, remove from the heat and whisk hard to ensure it does not split. It should become a thick custard. Pass the custard through a sieve into the chilled bowl and stir for a few minutes to cool it as quickly as possible. Add the remaining chilled cream and whisk until lightly whipped.

Pierce a hole in the side of the doughnuts and pipe the filling into the centre, then serve.

TWO CHOCOLATE FROSTINGS

MAKES ENOUGH TO COAT & FILL 25 DOUGHNUTS

milk cooking chocolate, broken into pieces	100g
double cream	100ml
Maldon sea salt	¼ tsp
peanut butter	50g
light muscovado sugar	50g

Melt the chocolate with the double cream and salt in a heatproof bowl set over a pan of gently simmering water, making sure the base of the bowl does not touch the water.

Divide the chocolate mixture between two bowls and add the peanut butter to one bowl and the sugar to the other bowl. Stir both mixtures thoroughly with a wooden spoon until smooth. Spoon the peanut butter frosting into a piping bag with a fine plain nozzle.

Pierce a hole in the side of the doughnuts and pipe the peanut butter frosting into the centre, then dip the top into the salted caramel frosting. Leave on a wire rack to set, then serve at room temperature.

Once cooled, these frostings will set hard and can be stored in the fridge for a few days.

— ICE CREAMS & SORBETS —

PRUNE & WHISKEY ICE CREAM

MAKES APPROXIMATELY 800ML

prunes, soaked in whiskey (see method)	75g
free-range egg yolks	80g (about 4 eggs)
caster sugar	140g
milk	500ml
double cream	100ml
whiskey	20ml

For this recipe use prunes that have been soaked in whiskey for 1 month.

Whisk together the egg yolks and 100g of the sugar in a large bowl using an electric hand whisk, until frothy and pale.

Put the milk, cream and remaining sugar into a pan and heat to 60°C. Slowly pour the hot milk mixture into the egg yolk/sugar mixture, stirring with the whisk. Cover the bowl, then put into the fridge and chill to 4°C. Once chilled, add the whiskey (ideally chilled to 4°C too), then transfer to an ice cream machine and churn according to the manufacturer's instructions. Fold in the prunes after churning.

PEANUT BUTTER ICE CREAM

MAKES APPROXIMATELY 800ML

egg yolks	40g (about 2 eggs)
caster sugar	125g
milk	500ml
double cream	50ml
peanut butter	100g
salt	a pinch

Whisk the egg yolks with 50g of the sugar in a large bowl.

Put the milk, cream, peanut butter, salt and remaining sugar into a pan and heat to 60°C. Slowly pour the hot milk mixture on to the egg yolks, stirring with the whisk. Cover the bowl, then put into the fridge and chill to 4°C.

Once chilled, transfer to an ice cream machine and churn according to the manufacturer's instructions.

SALTED CARAMEL
ICE CREAM

MAKES 1 LITRE

milk	300ml
double cream	300ml
milk chocolate	50g
free-range egg yolks	6
light muscovado sugar	150g
Maldon sea salt	1 tsp

Put the milk, cream and chocolate in a saucepan over a medium heat and bring to a simmer.

Whisk together the egg yolks, sugar and salt in a large bowl using an electric hand whisk, until they have doubled in volume.

Pour the hot milk mixture on to the egg yolk mixture and stir to combine. Pour through a fine sieve and leave to cool. Once cooled, transfer to an ice cream machine and churn according to the manufacturer's instructions.

RASPBERRY SORBET

MAKES APPROXIMATELY 500ML

fresh raspberries	1kg
lemon juice, to taste	
caster sugar	225g
water	375ml

First, make a raspberry purée. Put the raspberries in a saucepan over a low heat and cook until they begin to break down. Increase the heat and bring to the boil. Add lemon juice to taste. Remove from the heat, pass through a fine sieve and leave to cool before refrigerating.

Pour 500g of the raspberry purée into a pan and add the sugar and water. Bring to the boil, then pass through a fine sieve and leave to cool.

Once cooled, transfer to an ice cream machine and churn according to the manufacturer's instructions.

WHITE PEACH SORBET

MAKES APPROXIMATELY 500ML

white-flesh peaches	500g
caster sugar	120g
water	170ml
lemon juice	15ml

Before you start, put the peaches into the fridge and chill to 4°C.

Put the sugar into a bowl. Heat the water in a pan to 60°C, then pour over the sugar. Cover the bowl, put into the fridge and chill to 4°C.

Pour the lemon juice into a container (use plastic or glass; do not use metal). It must be large enough to hold the remaining ingredients.

Leaving the skins on, juice the cold peaches and immediately pour the juice into the container of lemon juice to prevent the juice from oxidizing. This must be done just prior to churning.

Add the cold sugar syrup to the container, stir to combine, then transfer to an ice cream machine and churn according to the manufacturer's instructions.

PEANUT BUTTER & CHOCOLATE TART

SINCE OPENING WE HAVE HAD
A NUMBER OF LOVE AFFAIRS
WITH ALL MANNER OF TRASHY
CHOCOLATE BARS, SOME JUST
WEEK-LONG FLINGS, OTHERS
BECOMING LENGTHY AND
FRUITFUL RELATIONSHIPS
AND SOME JUST TOO FILTHY AND
WRONG TO REPEAT. JUST LIKE
OUR 'SNICKERS' MESS, THIS
TART IS THE BEAUTIFUL LOVE-
CHILD OF ONE OF THE MORE
LONG-LIVED RELATIONSHIPS.

TRY GOING OVER THE SURFACE
OF THE PORTIONED TART WITH
A BLOWTORCH TO BRING BACK
ITS FULL GLOSS.

SERVES 10–12

butter	100g
cobnuts or hazelnuts	40g
chocolate biscuits (we use Oreos)	130g
smooth peanut butter	230g
caster sugar	40g
Maldon sea salt	5g
dark chocolate (70% cocoa solids)	250g
double cream	250ml
clotted cream	50ml
olive oil	15ml

Heat the oven to 200°C/400°F/gas mark 6.

Melt 40g of the butter in a pan. Put the
nuts and biscuits into a blender and blitz
to a powder, then add the melted butter and
combine. Press firmly and evenly into the
bottom of a 25cm diameter loose-bottomed
tart tin. Bake in the oven for 3–4 minutes,
then remove and leave to set.

Put the peanut butter and sugar into a bowl.
Melt the remaining 60g of butter in a pan,
add to the bowl and whisk until thick and
ribboning. Stir in the salt, then pour the
mixture into the tart tin on top of the
biscuit base and put into the fridge to set.

Make a ganache by melting the chocolate in
a heatproof bowl set over a pan of gently
simmering water, making sure the base of
the bowl does not touch the water. Remove
from the heat, add the cream and clotted
cream and stir until smooth and glossy.
Add the olive oil and stir again until
shiny and emulsified. Pour the ganache over
the peanut butter layer and leave to cool,
then refrigerate for 2 hours, or until set.
Serve with Raspberry Sorbet (see page 271).

— RHUBARB & LEMON TART —

WHEN THE FORCED RHUBARB SEASON STARTS IN JANUARY WE GO A BIT CRAZY IN THE RESTAURANT, WITH MESSES, PICKLES, JAMS, CHEESECAKES, TARTS, SORBETS AND BIG POACHING SESSIONS KEEPING THE PASTRY SECTION HAPPY. THIS IS A CLASSIC LEMON TART GIVEN A RHUBARB MAKEOVER, AND MAKES FOR A VERY CLEAN DESSERT AFTER SOME PIG.

SERVES 12

lemons	4
forced pink rhubarb	500g
caster sugar	300g
free-range eggs	9
double cream	300ml
seeds from 1 vanilla pod	

TOPPING

unsalted butter	300g
icing sugar, sifted	190g
eggs, beaten	2
plain flour	560g

First, make the pastry. Beat the butter and icing sugar in a mixing bowl until just beginning to come together. Mix in the eggs slowly, until thoroughly combined, scraping down the sides of the bowl as you go.

Carefully add half the flour and mix to a smooth paste, making sure not to overmix, then add the remaining flour and mix gently until a light dough is formed.

Wrap the dough in clingfilm and refrigerate for at least 2 hours before using.

Finely grate the zest of the lemons directly into a large bowl and set aside. Juice the lemons and set aside 175ml of juice.

Put the rhubarb through a centrifugal juicer and set aside 175ml of juice.

Place the rhubarb pulp, the leftover rhubarb juice, the leftover lemon juice and 50g of the caster sugar in a small pan. Cook down gently over a low heat for 10–15 minutes to make a rhubarb compote as thick and as dry as possible, trying not to let it catch. Set aside.

Roll out the pastry on a lightly floured surface as thinly as possible. Use it to line a 25cm diameter loose-bottomed tart tin. Place the pastry case in the fridge for 10 minutes to firm up.

Meanwhile, heat the oven to 200°C/400°F/ gas mark 6.

Line the pastry case with greaseproof paper and fill with baking beans. Blind bake for 15 minutes, or until the edges just start to colour. Remove the paper and beans and bake for a further 5 minutes, or until the base is dry. Remove from the oven and reduce the temperature to 130°C/260°F/gas mark 1.

Spread a thin layer of rhubarb compote over the base of the pastry case and flatten.

Add the eggs to the bowl containing the lemon zest, then whisk together with the remaining caster sugar, cream, vanilla seeds and reserved lemon and rhubarb juices. Pour this mixture carefully into the pastry case over the rhubarb compote layer. Bake in the oven for 40 minutes, or until just set. Allow to cool and fully set before serving.

STICKY BOURBON & COLA PUDDING

SERVES 12

dates, pitted and chopped	250g
prunes, pitted and chopped	250g
cola	750ml
unsalted butter	165g
maple or light muscovado sugar	250g
large free-range eggs	4
self-raising flour	650g
baking powder	10g
bicarbonate of soda	10g
Maldon sea salt	1 tsp

BOURBON CARAMEL SAUCE

milk chocolate	100g
unsalted butter	250g
maple or light muscovado sugar	250g
double cream	250ml
Maldon sea salt	¾ tsp
bourbon	75ml

BASED ON STICKY TOFFEE PUDDING, A QUINTESSENTIAL BRITISH DESSERT, THIS RECIPE GRACIOUSLY BASTARDIZES IT WITH A NOT-SO-GRACIOUS DOSE OF BOURBON AND COLA.

NO MATTER WHAT DESSERTS ARE ON THE MENU, THIS HAS THE KNACK OF OUTSELLING THEM. IT'S STICKY TOFFEE PUDDING IN OVERDRIVE, JUST TOO MUCH OF A TEMPTATION FOR ANYONE WHO HAS EVER HAD A MOMENT WITH, OR FALLEN COMPLETELY FOR, A STICKY TOFFEE PUDDING IN THEIR LIFE.

FOR THIS RECIPE YOU WILL NEED A 27–30CM DIAMETER SPRINGFORM CAKE TIN, LINED WITH GREASEPROOF PAPER SO THAT NONE OF THE PRECIOUS SAUCE CAN LEAK OUT.

Line a 27–30cm-diameter springform cake tin with greaseproof paper.

To make the bourbon caramel sauce, put the chocolate, butter and sugar into a pan and heat gently until melted. Take off the heat and whisk in the cream, salt and bourbon. Pour some of the sauce into the base of the tin and chill it in the fridge for 20 minutes. Set aside the rest of the sauce and keep warm.

Put the chopped dates and prunes into a pan with the cola and simmer over a low heat for 5 minutes. Meanwhile, using a free-standing mixer, beat together the butter and muscovado sugar. Mix in the eggs gradually, followed by the flour and baking powder. Add the bicarbonate of soda and salt to the hot date and prune mix, then add the mixture to the batter.

Heat the oven to 170°C/325°F/gas mark 3.

Pour the batter into the chilled tin, then bake in the oven for 40 minutes, or until risen and just cooked through.

Remove from the oven and make holes in the crust of the pudding with a skewer. Heat a little more sauce and pour over the top, then return the pudding to the oven for 5 minutes.

Turn out and serve with more sauce and clotted cream or ice cream.

BOURBON BABA

ORIGINALLY A SOBER AND DRY POLISH CAKE, IN THE EARLY NINETEENTH CENTURY THE BABA MADE ITS WAY TO FRANCE WHERE PÂTISSIERS INTRODUCED IT TO SYRUPS AND GLAZES, AND THE 'BABA AU RHUM' OR 'RUM BABA' WAS BORN. IT IS NOW A FRENCH CLASSIC, AND THE SAVARIN DOUGH WITH WHICH IT IS MADE IS A FUNDAMENTAL OF FRENCH PÂTISSERIE. THIS RECIPE OMITS THE BOOZY SOAKED FRUITS THAT OFTEN APPEAR IN RUM BABAS AND TRADES IN RUM FOR BOURBON. IF FOR SOME REASON BOURBON DOES NOT TURN YOU ON, USE RUM. BABAS CAN BE TRICKY LITTLE THINGS TO GET RIGHT.

MAKES 8

strong white flour	125g
salt	pinch
dried yeast	5g
eggs	3
maple syrup	10ml
unsalted butter, melted	75g

SYRUP

maple syrup	200ml
water	100ml
vanilla pod, split	1
bourbon	100ml
finely grated zest and juice of 1 lemon	
finely grated zest and juice of 1 orange	
finely grated zest and juice of 1 lime	

GLAZE

apricot conserve	100g
water	25ml

In a large mixing bowl, mix together the flour, salt, yeast, eggs and maple syrup, then beat for 5 minutes, until the mixture becomes a smooth batter. Pour the melted butter slowly into the batter in a fine stream, beating to fully incorporate. Continue to beat for another 5 minutes, until the savarin dough is completely smooth and free of any lumps. Leave the dough in the mixing bowl, covered, for 45 minutes, until doubled in size.

Knock back the dough. (When you first make a batch, the dough will probably seem far too wet — don't be tempted to add flour when knocking back the dough after it proves, as it can result in an overly 'cakey' baba that will please nobody.) Transfer to a piping bag and divide the batter between eight dariole moulds, putting roughly 30g into each one. The moulds need be no more than half full, as the dough will rise. Leave to prove at room temperature for 30–45 minutes, until the dough has doubled in size again. It will be bulging at this stage.

Heat the oven to 180°C/350°F/gas mark 4 and bake the babas for 12–15 minutes, until golden brown. Once baked, remove them from the moulds and leave to cool.

To make the syrup, put all syrup ingredients into a pan and bring to the boil. Reduce to a simmer for 15 minutes, then remove from the heat and leave for 20 minutes to cool slightly.

Add the babas to the syrup, turning them to make sure they are evenly covered. Remove them from the syrup and refrigerate on a wire rack until needed.

To make the apricot glaze, put the apricot conserve into a small pan with the water and warm through, stirring. To serve, brush the babas evenly with the glaze, then serve in a few more tablespoons of the syrup with ice cream and poached fruits.

SMOKED PEACHES

WHEN BEAUTIFULLY RIPE PEACHES ARE COOKED LIKE THIS, THEY NEED VERY LITTLE HELP. IF COOKED WELL THE SKINS PEEL OFF WITH BARELY ANY EFFORT AT ALL, WHICH IN ITSELF MAKES THE WHOLE THING WORTHWHILE — SUCH IS THE SATISFACTION OF A PERFECTLY NAKED PEACH! WE SERVED THEM AS IS, BUT WHEN WE DISCOVERED PIMM'S SORBET WE COULD THINK OF NO BETTER PARTNER FOR IT THAN A WARM, SMOKED PEACH. VERY LITTLE SMOKE IS NEEDED FOR THIS RECIPE; JUST A HINT IS ALL YOU WANT.

SERVES 4

ripe peaches	4
Maldon sea salt	pinch

Prepare a barbecue for direct grilling over medium heat — around 150°C is best — and add a small handful of wood chunks (see page 112). Place a sheet of buttered paper on the grill, butter side up, then place the peaches on top and close the lid. Cook for 20 minutes, until the peaches are just soft to the touch.

Remove the peaches from the barbecue and leave to cool for 5 minutes. The skin should peel off without much effort, though the very base of the peach may need to be removed with a knife, as the skin on the surface touching the butter paper is less forgiving.

Serve the peaches with a pinch of sea salt and Pimm's Sorbet (see below).

PIMM'S SORBET

MAKES APPROXIMATELY 500ML

good-quality lemonade	400ml
mint leaves	10
caster sugar	180g
juice of ½ a large orange	
juice of ½ a large lemon	
cucumber, juiced	2cm piece
fresh strawberries, quartered	2
Pimm's	100ml

Put the lemonade into a large pan and add the mint leaves. Heat slowly over a low heat to 40°C, then add the sugar. Stir until the sugar has completely dissolved, then remove from the heat.

Add the orange juice, lemon juice, cucumber juice and strawberries to the lemonade mixture. Let the mixture cool to 4°C in the refrigerator. When cold, remove the mint leaves and strawberries, then transfer to an ice cream machine and churn according to the manufacturer's instructions. After 4 minutes add the Pimm's and continue to churn until the sorbet is frozen.

INDEX

Bold page numbers indicate the main recipe.

ACKNOWLEDGEMENTS

As with anything that grows from nothing, Pitt Cue has relied on a lot of luck and a lot of help. We are incredibly fortunate to have amazing people involved in Pitt Cue and to have had so many people support us when we first started. The team in Soho have put up with one of the smallest restaurants known to man and played a huge part in creating the recipes in this book, especially Fran, Thea, Neil, Swanny and Chris, all of whom have been integral in bringing it to fruition. Looking back from when we first decided to buy a trailer there are a ridiculous number of people who should take credit for where we are now:

The Adams clan in Pitt for absolute awesomeness on all fronts: Mother Adams for putting up with lots of hairy pigs at home. Georgie Adams, Pitt Cue's first employee and creator of beautiful illustrations. And to Augustus, Empress, Bacon Head and Juno: Pitt's finest pigs.

Robbie Bargh for making the introductions to get us that first pitch on the South Bank.

Charlie, Frank and Jackson Boxer for the idea, inspiration and support, and for housing the trailer, the smoker, Tom, Georgie and Jamie.

Sam Burge, one of the few people as white as Tom, for looking after the pigs in Pitt and babysitting the trailer all winter long.

Matt Chatfield for huge dedication to bringing Cornish produce and Warrens Butchers to London, and for being very Cornish: a food hero.

Jonathan Downey for making shit happen all summer long, and bringing the vibes.

David Ezrine for constant egg supply, showing us the importance of 'no peeking' and more awesomeness. Hater of flan.

Hawksmoor for giving Richard freedom to pursue outside interests.

Peder Henriksson. There from before the start: the bearded Swede – scourge of the Baltic.

Anne Hynes for understanding barbecue and allowing us to be part of the Festival of Britain 60th Anniversary celebrations.

Nick Kelvin for bringing brilliant smokers to London.

Jeremy Lee for kisses and fondles.

Sean O'Neil at Keveral Farm for being an all-round legend and growing things we never knew existed. James George, for putting up with lots of shit, helping us all the way and being a general geezer. Dermot, for putting up with even more shit than James on a daily basis.

Erica Page for her blackboard writing skills and for putting up with Simon.

Barry Skarin for whipping us all into shape, a fountain of knowledge and reassurance. We'd be going backwards if it weren't for your bollockings.

Andy and Lee Stevens for their investment and support in getting Soho off the ground.

The team at Speciality – Raj, Nic & Adriano – for keeping us awash with bourbon from Day One.

The whole gang at Warrens Butchers in Launceston, Cornwall. Especially Phillip Warren, Ian Warren, and Rhea Warren, the collective 'Meat Bible' of Cornwall, for putting up with some ridiculous requests and rearing some beautiful animals. You guys have taught us so much in such a short space of time and continue to set the precedent. We owe so much to you.

Zeren Wilson, the walking restaurant guide and bible of wine. There from the start, the catalyst.

Paul Winch-Furness for beautiful photos and questionable shirts.

Charlie Hart, Cornish Pig Lord.

Pitt Cue Co. Cookbook

By

Tom Adams, Simon Anderson, Jamie Berger and Richard Turner

An Hachette UK Company
www.hachette.co.uk

First published in Great Britain in 2013 by Mitchell Beazley,
an imprint of Octopus Publishing Group Ltd,
Endeavour House, 189 Shaftesbury Avenue,
London WC2H 8JY
www.octopusbooks.co.uk

Reprinted in 2013 (twice)

British Library Cataloguing-in-Publication Data.
A catalogue record for this book is available from the British Library.

Publisher Stephanie Jackson
Deputy art director Yasia Williams-Leedham
Jacket and book design Samuel Muir
Photographer Paul Winch-Furness (except page 16 middle right and 17 centre Thomas Bowles)
Illustrations Georgie Adams (except page 116 Samuel Muir)
Senior editor Sybella Stephens
Assistant production manager Lucy Carter

ISBN: 978 1 84533 756 8
Printed and bound in China

Simon

Tom

Richard

Jamie

1 Newburgh Street, Soho, London W1F 7RB

www.pittcue.co.uk

@PittCueCo